# Self-Editing for the Successful Pre-Law Student

# Self-Editing for the Successful Pre-Law Student

**Elizabeth Huntoon Coursen**

Published by OrangeBlossomPublishing.com
Sarasota, Florida

ISBN: 978-1-951158-07-1

www.EditNATION.com
Liz@EditNATION.com



Also by Elizabeth Huntoon Coursen:

*Brunswick and Bowdoin College* (2009)

*The Complete Biography Workbook* (2010)

*Self-Editing for the Self-Published Author* (2012)

*The Book Tourist: Seven Steps to a Wildly Successful Book Tour* (2013)

*Shade in the Sunshine State: Reflections on Segregation in Florida* (2014)

*Self-Editing for the Modern Author* (2014)

*Self-Editing for Content Writers* (2014)

*Before You Even Open Your Mouth: The Writing Guide For Professional Speakers* (2015)

*Self-Editing for the Successful Student* (2017)

*Self-Editing for Today's Business Owner* (2017)

*Write* AMERICAN! *Business Writing in American English* (India edition) (2017)

*Write* AMERICAN! *for the Successful Student* (India edition) (2017)

*Write* AMERICAN! *For Marketing and Sales Professionals* (India edition) (2017)

With the exception of *The Complete Biography Workbook*, which is available only through the author, and *Self-Editing for the Self-Published Author*, which has been republished as *Self-Editing for the Modern Author*, all books are available on Amazon.com.

Coming soon:

*Self-Editing for the Effective Nonprofit* (2022)

*Real Estate Writing Best Practices* (2022)

**Dedication.**

To my Aunt Dede,

for being such a wonderful role model

in so many ways.

**Acknowledgments.**

I would like to thank my mother, Susan Kirkconnell Coursen, who was a superb editor.

## Table of Contents

# Introduction.

**Question:** What's your big goal right now?

**Answer:** Getting into the law school of your choice.

So, the answer to the question above is simple: Your big goal right now is to get great grades.

**Truth:** Great grades lead to a great law school.

**Truth:** A great law school leads to the job you want.

**Truth:** You need great grades.

Great. This book is going to help you big-time. In school and out, understanding punctuation and grammar is going to be huge. Your understanding of punctuation and grammar rules is going to give you a competitive edge because the gatekeepers—your teachers and professors—will stutter in excitement and practically foam at the mouth when you turn in work that is exemplary.

If there's one TRUTH about life, my friends, it's this: First impressions count. First impressions matter. Like it or not, people make assumptions about you, your ability, experience, seriousness, knowledge, and the value of your ideas by how you choose to represent yourself—in person and, believe it, in writing. Your authority can hinge on how you look. You know it, I know it, so why beat around the bush about it?

The sad thing is that lots of people seem blithely unaware of how important it is to use proper and correct punctuation. It's crazy!

I got the idea to write *Self-Editing for the Successful Pre-Law Student* because I've been embroiled in a nasty lawsuit with a real jerk of a lawyer who can't write his way out of a paper sack. The writing mistakes he's made (and we have just gotten out of the gate) have been *epic.*

However, the bad writing extends to everyone involved, from the judicial assistants, to the receptionists, to the law clerks, to the judges (yes!).

One afternoon, while researching what would eventually be a 67-page petition to the Second District Court of Appeal, a vision of my college days floated into my mind, back when I managed to graduate from a pretty decent school as an English major. I graduated with an English degree and a pretty decent grasp of American English punctuation, but my knowledge wasn't rock solid, if you know what I mean. I did a lot of hoping, a lot of guessing. Nobody bothered to take me aside and say, "Liz, here's a book you need. You are smart and have important things to share. The way you convey your messages is almost as important as the message itself. In fact, if you don't express yourself correctly, no one will read what you write."

Nobody said that to me, so I didn't think it. If nothing has changed since then (and it seems things might have even gotten worse), then young people are out and about like I was out and about: with a pretty decent grasp of basic American English, but not a rock-solid one.

Suddenly, I had a brilliant idea: if I can write a brand new style guide that illustrates the rules, that shows pre-law students how to write clearly, persuasively, and correctly, avoiding the pesky punctuation and grammar mistakes I see all day, every day, in court and on the internet—why, if I could put all the rules in one place and share the guide with those students, maybe they could avoid all the mistakes I made! Hey, we can all be thought leaders together!

That moment was the genesis of this book. It's all here: where to place a comma, when to use a semicolon and not parentheses, the vast gulf between a dash and a hyphen, and how to put quotation marks around darn near everything. Proper use of punctuation in your writing is *de rigueur*: as pre-law student it's simply a given that you will learn to punctuate things correctly. If you think your paralegals will be responsible for catching your mistakes, think again!

*Self-Editing for the Successful Pre-Law Student* is meant to do one thing: to ensure your writing is professional and precise. This book will focus on two aspects of your content: its punctuation/grammar and its readability.

Chapter 1 is all about punctuation and grammar. The purpose of punctuation is to convey your message clearly. Every time a reader is confused, every time a reader stops or hesitates and has to try to figure out what it was that you just tried to say, you've failed as a writer. Using punctuation properly is the key to properly conveying your message. It seems to me that every writer of American English should have a good grounding in basic punctuation and grammar rules—this "good grounding" should—in my opinion—come with the territory.

Then there's the issue of readability, which we discuss in Chapter 2. Here we discuss your choice of and use of words. One of the main goals of *Self-Editing for the Successful Pre-Law Student* is not to homogenize your voice (perish the thought) or even to fiddle (very much) with how you choose to express yourself, it is to encourage you to seek out *le mot juste* in your writing. The best writers—the ones professors (and judges!) love to read—are passionate in their pursuit of the proper word, the right word, the absolute perfect word in every circumstance, and I'll show you how to examine writing samples so you can do just that with your own work.

As you continue to write, let me encourage you to *read*. Take your favorite books off the shelf (literally or figuratively) and read them slowly. Linger over commas and semicolons. Pay attention to capitalization. You may never have paid any attention to the role punctuation plays in the story: now is the time to sit up and take notice. Two authors I recommend as exemplars of good writing are Stephen King and Tom Clancy. King and Clancy are decidedly *au courant*, and both authors manage to convey sophisticated dialog and complicated plots with superb use of words and correct use of punctuation. Mr. Clancy's plots weave action with information, incorporating abbreviations and other stylistic elements less likely to be seen in many books, so there's a great deal to be learned from a careful reading of a Tom Clancy novel. Mr. King's deft turn of phrase and in-the-moment narrative style is an unbeatable combination (as his sales attest). Another wonderful author whose content I use extensively in this book is E. F. Benson, brilliant author of *Make Way for Lucia*. If it sounds quaint and British, it's Benson!

This book also contains many very "modern" sentences, ripped from the pages of the internet, which, sad to say, are demonstrative of the low level of writing in general nowadays. I'm not sure if people don't know the rules, or know the rules and just don't care, as though for whatever reason the rules no longer apply. I'm convinced of one thing: the surest way to ruin your credibility is to not know basic American English punctuation and grammar rules. In other words, you could have the most important message in the world, but without the gift wrap and the big, fat bow, your wonderful message won't reach your audience.

Two more things, from someone who knows.

First, take a few typing classes. Accurate typing is going to make a huge difference in how your written work is received by your professors.

Second, join Toastmasters International. I'm confident that there is a Toastmasters club on your campus. Here you will learn to speak correctly and compellingly in a supportive and engaged environment. Toastmasters isn't just "game-changing": Toastmasters is *life*-changing.

Perfection = Professionalism! Professionalism = Great grades!

Master the rules set forth in this book. Get a reputation as the go-to person in your class for punctuation and grammar questions. Be the authority. Read *everything* and edit *everyone*. By purchasing this book you are well on your way to having an excellent grasp of American English, and you will use our beautiful, remarkable language with confidence and clarity. Writing well is an absolutely amazing experience, a total thrill.

And I promise that using this book will make you a subject-matter expert. Using this book will help you become a true thought leader. And I know that using this book will take you where you want to go.

And—last thing—this is fun! Just watch and see!

Best wishes, be brave, and...make it perfect!

*Liz Coursen*
Sarasota, Florida, 2022

PS. As I mentioned, I use many sentences in this edition that are taken directly from internet content. Most of the time, I have changed identifying names, whether personal or business. Sometimes, however, if someone is a self-proclaimed "expert" litigator or if law firm's website contains typos or other problematic writing, as a rule, I put the writing in as it stands, warts and all. Listen, it's not like I'm taking content from a mom-and-pop pizza parlor here; the websites whose content I use in this book are major players, one and all. I have no patience whatsoever with people who brag about their successes and their advanced degrees and yet put their imprimatur on sloppy content. They might be major players, but I will tell you one thing: money doesn't automatically make you a thought leader!

Oh, and by the way, I blog about editing issues and post punctuation and grammar quizzes at EditNATION.com. Come join me for some fun!

Oh, and one more thing. I don't address the issue of footnotes. The best advice I can give you is to ask your teacher/professor what style he or she wants to see, and use that style.

Oh, and last thing: I was being snarky when I used the terms "thought leader" and "subject-matter expert," two of the most overused phrases in the English language. Clichés...*boo*!!!

Truly last thing: The Second District Court of Appeal just agreed to hear my petition and granted me oral argument. I like to think the judges liked both my argument *and* they liked the overall appearance of my petition, because this jerk of a lawyer (40 years' experience!) put up quite a fight against both!

## The TOP TEN editing issues.

Master these rules, and you've won most of the battle!

**1. *It's* versus *its*.**

This is a biggie.

It's = it is. It can also be the contraction of *it has*.

*Its* is the possessive of *it*.

**2. Quotation marks.**

In American English, both single and double quotation marks always go *outside* periods and commas. There are no exceptions. Hear my voice in your head: There. Are. No. Exceptions.

**3. Hyphens versus dashes.**

A hyphen is a mark of joining; a dash is a mark of separation. They are two completely different punctuation marks, with totally different roles.

A hyphen ( - ) is not a dash ( — ). Only a dash is a dash.

**4. Colons and lists.**

Do not use a colon after *include, includes, including.*

Do not use a colon after *for example.*

Do not use a colon following a preposition, like *of* or *in*, or following a prepositional phrase, like *such as.*

**5. The comma splice and the run-on sentence.**

A *comma splice* and a run-on sentence happen when two sentences are jammed together without correct punctuation. You basically have three options:

- keep the sentences separated and write them as two sentences
- use a conjunction (like *and*) and a comma to join the sentences
- use a semicolon to join the sentences

Examples:

She played poorly, he didn't play much better. (comma splice)

She played poorly and he didn't play much better. (run-on)

She played poorly, and he didn't play much better. (correct)

She played poorly; he didn't play much better. (correct)

**6. Right word, wrong spelling.**

Two words that sound the same but are spelled differently are called *homonyms*. This book contains a comprehensive list of homonyms. The tricky part is that spell-check *will not* pick up an incorrect use; that's *your* job.

**7. Capitalization.**

There's much too much capitalization going on nowadays. If a word isn't the first word in a sentence or line, a proper noun, or part of a proper noun phrase, then *it is not capitalized.* The seasons aren't capitalized. The word *clients* is never capitalized. If two proper nouns come together (Stanford and Harvard, for example), you write *Stanford and Harvard universities*, not *Universities*. Read the Capitalization section for more.

**8. The serial comma.**

I'm for it. If it helps one person understand your message, it ought to be used in every circumstance. Use it. Punctuation and grammar is an all-or-nothing proposition.

**9. Noun-verb-pronoun agreement.**

A singular noun takes a singular verb takes a singular pronoun.

A plural noun takes a plural verb takes a plural pronoun.

**10. Editorial/creative continuity.**

Rules and usage have to be the same, page after page after page.

## Words and phrases whose time has come...and gone.

One of the things about being a thought leader is avoiding clichés. Here is a list of words and expressions that you should consider *not* using.

Thought leader (using this phrase is the sure sign of someone who is not)

Align/misalign

To take something "to the next level" or "to a different level"

To go up or down "a notch"

To "reach out"

To "go missing"

Glom

Awesome (God is awesome. Mother Nature is awesome. End of story.)

"You guys" (*especially* when addressing a woman older than, say, 50)

Deep dive

Scale, scalability

Optimize

Rad

Best practices

Skill set

Tool box/tool set (*toolset* is worse)

Way better, way more

Connect the dots

Hacks

Buzz

Robust

Brain dump

Leverage

Buy-in

Riff

Majorly (as an adverb)

Stakeholder

Drill down

Ahead of the curve

At the end of the day (Thank You to my author friend Jane V. Blanchard!)

Craft (as a verb)

Disruptive

Double down

Dude (Do not, do not, do not call me a dude!)

Spend (as a noun)

Onboarding (as a verb)

Task (as a verb)

Impactful

Stoke (used in anything other than "I stoked the fire" context)

Score (used in anything other than a sports context)

Über (as in über important)

Up-level (Are you kidding me?)

Overwhelm (As a noun? Nuts. Just nuts.)

Rock, as in totally

Totally

# Chapter 1. Punctuation and Grammar.

## Part 1: Types of words.

To properly punctuate a sentence, you must first understand the “building blocks” of sentence structure. The good news is that you learned all of this already, somewhere in the not-so-distant past, so the following information will be in the nature of a review....So, let’s review!

There are nine types of words. They are:

Adjectives
Adverbs
Articles
Conjunctions
Interjections
Nouns
Prepositions
Pronouns
Verbs

## Adjectives.

An *adjective*, as we all know, serves to describe and specify a noun.

Example: The car was fast.

Question: What kind of car was it? Answer: fast.

Example: After judicious comparison, Liz decided her dream car was an Amethyst Metallic Porsche Turbo S Cabriolet.

Here we have two nouns: car and Porsche.

What kind of car was it? Liz's "dream" car. "Dream" is the first adjective.

What kind of Porsche was it? An Amethyst Metallic Turbo S Cabriolet.

## Adverbs.

An *adverb* describes a verb, an adjective, or another adverb, completing the questions of *how, how much, when*, or *where.*

Examples:

She ate slowly. ("Slowly" modifies the verb "ate.")

I play tennis very well. ("Very well" modifies "play." *Not* "She plays tennis very good. "Good" is an adjective; "well" is a adverb.)

A *conjunctive adverb* coordinates clauses in a sentence. Use a semicolon before a conjunctive adverb, and follow with a comma. *After all, also, as a result, besides, consequently, finally, for example, furthermore, however, in addition, in fact, in other words, incidentally, indeed, instead, likewise, nevertheless, next, nonetheless, on the contrary, on the other hand, otherwise, meanwhile, moreover, still, then,* and *thus* are examples of conjunctive adverbs.

Never hyphenate an adverb that ends in *-ly.* This is *incorrect:*

His professor discovered that he used previously-written material.

## Articles.

*Articles* identify a noun, as opposed to describing it. In English, the definite article is *the*, and the indefinite articles are "a" and *an.*

## Conjunctions.

A *conjunction* joins words, phrases, and clauses. There are two kinds of conjunctions: *coordinating* conjunctions, like *and, but, or, nor, for, yet,* and *so*, and *subordinate* conjunctions, such as *after, although, as, because, before, even if, even though, if, in order that, once, next, provided that, rather than, since, so that, supposing, than, that, though, unless, until, what, when, where, whereas, wherever, whether, which, while, who,* and *why.*

Conjunctions have different "strengths," and establish varying degrees of relationship between things, people, or situations. Many conjunctions also have other meanings (*since,* for example, is a preposition that can be used to express "from the time that"), so be careful to use the best conjunction in each circumstance.

**Style note:** I have begun to notice a lot of what I call the "'or' equivalency" in modern writing. The "'or' equivalency" happens when the author joins two synonyms or near-synonyms with "or": coerced or forced, beaten or flogged, deserted or left, eating grass or chewing cud, clients or customers, handbag or purse, negative or harmful, job or project. A subset of this rule is when two very similar words are used, words like purple or white, wall or gates, *Forbes* or *The Wall Street Journal.*

Here's a good example:

Use social inbox to set up streams to find people who are searching for a problem you help them solve or the solution you provide.

What is the difference between you helping people solve a problem or you providing a solution? Aren't they basically the same thing?

How about "knowledge" and "expertise"? Aren't they pretty much the same thing?

Here's another example:

The team lacked a background in marketing and had no formal strategy on how to connect with their users or visitors.

Sure, there's a difference between *users* and *visitors,* though what it is isn't made clear in this sentence. But is the difference enough to have both words in the same sentence? Why not say *visitors* and leave it at that?

Here's another example:

The majority of our web leads were either garbage or spam.

There's a real fine line between garbage and spam; in fact, all spam *is* garbage. Since the sentence is specifically about the internet and *spam* is an internet-specific word, I'd go with spam.

So, this sentence would be better if it read: "The majority of our web leads were spam."

A related issue is the "'and' equivalency," which is not nearly as irksome as the "'or' equivalency," but wastes space nonetheless: isolation *and* loneliness, drudgery *and* tedium, picky *and* choosy, helpful *and* useful.

Example: If you're competitive, motivated and driven, this role might just be for you.

If you wanted to say someone was "tall, dark, and handsome," well, those are three adjectives that mean three very different things. The adjectives *competitive, motivated*, and *driven* are more alike than they are different, so using one would have been enough.

And yet another example:

"We were all very anxious and worried."

What is the difference between "anxious" and "worried"? Not enough, my friends, not enough.

Still, if the "'and' equivalency" is bad, the "'or' equivalency" is worse. I do not know why the "'or' equivalency" is happening (perhaps people are aping a sort of cover-all-your-bases-or-you'll-get-sued legalistic style or perhaps they are airing their extensive vocabularies), but it's something to be avoided because it's confusing and slows the narrative down to a crawl. Remember: The conjunction *and* is inclusive; *or* implies a choice.

**For more on Conjunctions, see the section about Commas.**

## Interjections.

An *interjection* is used to interrupt the flow of a sentence to introduce an emotion of excitement, fear, surprise, and so on.

Example: I drove my Porsche like a maniac, and boy! was it fun!

## Nouns.

A *noun* is used to name actions, ideas, persons, places, and things. Typically, words that follow articles ("a," *an*, and *the*) are nouns: a cat, an elephant, the dog.

It is critical that a noun and its pronoun and verb agree in quantity. This is incorrect:

A witness in a deposition normally has their attorney present.

"A witness" is singular, but "their" is a plural pronoun. Sloppy.

Correct: A witness in a deposition normally has his or her attorney present.

Correct: Witnesses in a deposition normally have their attorney present.

Typically, when two nouns are joined by *and,* the verb is plural.

Example: The china and the silver were my grandmother's.

An exception to this rule would occur if the compound subject is referring to a single person or a unit.

Examples:

The author and the publisher is Liz Coursen.

Peaches and cream is my favorite summertime dessert.

Subjects joined by *or*, either/or, and neither/nor generally take a singular verb:

Liz or her assistant takes calls between 8 a.m. and 5 p.m. during the week.

Either Liz or her assistant takes calls during the week.

However, if one subject is singular and one is plural, the verb generally agrees with the subject closest to it.

Examples:

Neither my demeanor nor my arguments were persuasive.

Neither my arguments nor my demeanor was persuasive.

Beware a sentence like the sentence that follows, which is incorrect:

The staff at the college receive a better deal than the professors.

## The Collective Noun Rule.

Sometimes you'll run into a noun that's called a *collective* noun; in other words, a noun that refers to (or can refer to) a group of people, but is treated as a unit (one). *Administration, audience, band, cast, chapter, choir, citizenry, clergy, club, committee, community, company, congregation, contingent, crew, detail, enemy, faction, faculty, family, flock, household, gang, generation, group, herd, jury, management, manufacturer, media, membership, mob, network, nonprofit, organization, panel, party, public, series, staff, syndicate, team, throng, tribe, trio, troop, troupe,* and *workforce* are all examples of collective nouns.

So, the sentence should properly read:

The staff at the college receives a better deal than the professors.

If you didn't mean the group as a unit, but the group as individuals, you could write:

The staff members receive a better deal than the professors.

Correct: The clergy believes in God.

Correct: The clergy members believe in God.

I've been thinking about *clientele*, and I've decided clientele is a collective noun. I know, sometimes you have to think about it!

A real problem for many people is noun-pronoun agreement when talking about businesses and organizations. A business is always singular and is an *it*. While you can say *we* and *our* when referring to your business and its employees, a business is a *that*, not a *who:* The business that did this, the company that located here, the organization that raised the bar. Always. Don't be afraid to rephrase if it feels awkward to follow this rule.

So, all these sentences are incorrect:

Google is a master of making/testing changes on their site.

Kiva goes beyond that in getting their existing community to help.

Zappos is online, so they have an almost unlimited inventory.

Xerox is beginning to benefit from their strategy to expand their services business.

"Even John Lobb, who is one of the most conservative companies in the world, they finally realized they have to step it up and start playing," he said. [Drop the "who is," too.]

No! No! No! A company is not a person. A company is an *it* or a *that*.

All these rules about companies apply to countries as well. A country is an *it*. This sentence, for example, is incorrect:

India is the second-largest exporter of OTC and generic medications to the United States, and their imports help to keep pharmaceutical costs in the States low for consumers.

India is an *it*, so the possessive pronoun should be *its*.

I find the *its* versus *it's* mistake so easy make when I'm typing that I can often be found muttering to myself, "Opposite of logic. Opposite of logic," whenever *I* double-check my use of *its* or *it's*.

There are plenty of words that are collective nouns but don't refer to people. One that comes immediately to mind is *arsenal*. Another is *fleet:* A fleet of volunteer bus drivers is helping people escape eastern Ukraine.

**Naturally, there are exceptions to the collective noun rule.**

An example of a collective noun that typically takes a plural verb and pronoun is *personnel.*

Other collective nouns to watch out for are *variety* and *number.* Preceded by the indefinite article "a," *variety* and *number* take a plural verb and pronoun.

Examples:

A staggering variety of cookies, pies, and desserts are offered.

A number of them are failing the class.

However, when *variety* and *number* are preceded by the definite article *the,* both become singular.

Examples:

The variety of offerings is staggering.

The number of people failing the class is astonishing.

Sometimes, what seems to be the subject of a sentence is really an adjective in disguise. For example, when a sentence talks about a portion of something, like *all, among, any, fraction, half, majority, many, most, none, percent, part,* and *some,* the object of the preposition (the *of* part), whether stated or implied, determines whether the verb is singular or plural. For example, *none* means no single one, in which case *none* would take a singular verb, unless *none* is used to mean no two or no amount, which would necessitate a plural verb.

Examples:

Many of the *postcards* were stolen. (Many of them were stolen.)

None of *it* was stolen. (No part was stolen.)

None of the *ministers* agree about how to properly celebrate Easter. (No *two* agree.)

Liz collects vintage postcards. Some are worth a lot of money. (Some of *them* are worth a lot.)

The collection was worth a lot. However, only some was valuable. (Some of *it* was valuable.)

Don't be confused by the introduction of a collective noun.

Example:

Many in the crowd were restless. (Many [of the people] in the crowd were restless.)

Another example of a noun that seems to be singular, refers to a group of people, and takes a plural noun is the name of a sports team: The Boston Bruins are exciting to watch.

**Beware!** The introduction of parentheses, commas, or dashes completely separates the information inside those marks, so you cannot count that information for purposes of verb conjunction or pronoun choice.

**Writing about a company.**

As discussed just now, a company, business, or organization is not a human. None of the personal pronouns, like *he, she, they, their, theirs,* or *yours* can be used in association with a single business entity. A company is an *it* or *that*, never a *who*, unless you are talking about the company and you, and then you can say *we, our,* and *ours*. When referring to a company's products, services, mission statement, snack bar, hierarchy, policies, or whatever, you write *its:* its exercise facilities, its policies, its profits.

You cannot write this: Uflex is a Sarasota based company who has grown to lead the design, development, and manufacturing of the Marine Steering and Control Systems.

A company is an *it* and a *that*, never a *who*.

(Additionally, there should be a hyphen between Sarasota and based; plus, as far as I know, Marine Steering and Control Systems is not a proper noun phrase, so none of those words should be capitalized. A bad sentence all around.)

All business entities are singular, one unit, and never a "they."

This sentence is so wrong:

The stated purpose of this motion was to "provide further support for a critical determining factor in this case, that Gulf Coast ... had ample administrative remedies which, for whatever reason, they chose to ignore." (And just look at that sloppy ellipsis!)

A company can be composed of smaller sections, of course, and it can have branches, or outlets, or locations, but the company itself can't be anything but singular.

When writing a company's name, be conscious of its spelling. Check and double-check *and* versus *ampersand* (&), *Company* versus *Co., Inc.* versus *Incorporated.* If a company has an uppercase letter in its name following the first letter (eBay comes to mind), then make sure you write the name the way the company spells it.

Lots of times people will forget a comma in a situation when they've written the name of a company in text, like this:

> He also held senior management roles in a decade long career with ADP Inc. where he contributed to the Global Account Management strategy, industry leading growth rates, and ADP's evolution to become one of the world's most successful multi-product SaaS providers.

There should be a comma after *Inc.*, in addition to hyphens in *decade-long* and *industry-leading.* I also think *evolution to become* is redundant: *evolution into* would have sufficed.

Forgetting an appropriate comma after an abbreviation is a very common mistake. The sentences below should have a comma after *Inc.* (Each of these sentences has other issues, which is not surprising. That second sentence is *especially* bad; read it and you'll see what I mean.)

Prior to this position, he was an Apple Fellow at Apple Computer, Inc. and sits on the board of BitPass, FilmLoop, and SimplyHired.

On November 22, 2011, he advised the board of directors the of Cyalume Technologies Holdings, Inc. that he intended to resign from the Board.

It's obvious no one read this sentence before publication. "The of"? Why is "board" capitalized? The missing comma is the least of this writer's worries.

*The Associated Press Stylebook* (*AP Stylebook*) says not to use a comma before Inc. or Ltd. Since there is no explanation to mull over, and, on the face of it, it doesn't really make sense, I say use a comma if that is the legal name of the business.

## Prepositions.

A *preposition* links a noun or pronoun to another word in a sentence and typically defines the relationship between the two. Words like *by, during, from, in, of, since, to,* and *under* are prepositions. A *prepositional phrase* (*such as, along with, in addition to*) is formed when a preposition and its object act as an adjective or adverb.

Examples:

An inspiration of purest ray serene seized Liz.

(*Of* links purest ray serene to inspiration.)

Before the trial, he rather unwisely bragged that it was in the bag.

(*In* links the bag to the trial.)

Never follow a preposition or prepositional phrase with a colon.

## Pronouns.

A *pronoun* is a word used as a substitute for a noun or, sometimes, another pronoun. A pronoun is used to avoid needless repetition. Without pronouns, sentences would look like this:

Liz loved to drive her Alfa Romeo—when the Alfa Romeo wasn't in the shop, anyway—because the Alfa Romeo looked as good as the Alfa Romeo was fast.

("It," not surprisingly, is an oft-used pronoun.)

A pronoun can be the subject of a verb, the possessor, or the object of a verb or a preposition. Common pronouns include *I, me, mine, us, ours, he, she, his, her, him, hers, they, their, theirs, them, we, who, whose, whom, you, your,* and *yours*. Pronouns can also be indefinite, as in *anyone, anybody, everybody, everyone, no one, someone,* and *whoever.*

Pronouns often act as the "placeholder" for a noun. For instance, if a person who is being addressed or the thing that is being referred to has been identified elsewhere (somewhere close, so there's no ambiguity), the question "Where did you park my Porsche?" can be stated as "Where is it parked?" (Or even "Where is it?") And in the sentence "It is too hot," the "it" is understood to mean either the temperature of some previously identified, obviously understood thing or the temperature in general.

A *relative pronoun* (*that, which, who/whom, whoever/whomever, whose*) introduces a relative clause, which can be either restrictive (essential to the meaning of the sentence) or nonrestrictive (extra information not essential to understanding the sentence). Both *who* and *that* can refer to a person, while *which* and *that* can refer to things.

For more on relative pronouns, see the "That vs. Who, Who vs. Whom, That vs. Which" section in Chapter 2.

Note: beware the ambiguous, dangling pronoun. Make sure your readers understand very clearly who or what you are referring to when you write *it, she, he, they,* and so on. Do not use "it" to refer to two or more things within the same paragraph. When the action involves two women, for example, be sure to make it clear which woman you are referring to when you write "her eyes." If there is the least little doubt, err on the side of giving your reader too much definite information, as opposed to not enough.

Here's a good example of how two, similar pronouns in a compound sentence can be confusing:

We know that sales and marketing are working towards the same goals, so why don't we better align their methods for following up leads and converting them to customers?

Here, we have *their* referring back to "sales and marketing," followed by *them*, which, as it turns out, does not refer to "sales and marketing" but to "leads."

How about this instead?

We know that sales and marketing are working towards the same goals, so why don't we better align their methods for following up leads and converting those leads into customers?

Nouns, verbs, and pronouns must always agree in quantity and, when appropriate, gender. A singular subject takes a singular verb and a singular pronoun. You cannot use a singular subject with a singular verb and a plural pronoun. Always make sure your subject agrees with your noun or pronoun.

For example, "anyone" is a singular pronoun. So is "everyone." You would never say something like "Everyone are there," which means you can't write "Everyone has their swimming gear with them." A sentence written "Anyone with any sense would have known to write their real name on the petition" is incorrect, because "their" is a plural pronoun. The sentence should be written "Anyone with any sense would have known to write his or her name on the petition." If that sounds stiff to you, then rewrite as "People with any sense would have known to write their name on the petition."

Here's good example of a sentence that needs to be entirely rewritten:

Everyone thinks their company is "disruptive" and their software is "intelligent" and "easy-to-use," and everyone thinks their financial projections are "conservative."

(One of the problems, which is discussed in the Hyphens section, is that this writer has hyphenated the phrase "easy to use" after the noun it is modifying, which is incorrect.)

One possibility for the previous sentence would be:

We all like to think that our companies are "disruptive" and our software is "intelligent" and "easy to use," and we all know that our financial projections are "conservative."

## Pronoun and antecedent agreement.

Don't panic: an "antecedent" is simply the word to which the pronoun refers. Noun-pronoun-verb agreement is the cornerstone of American English. A pronoun agrees in number and gender with its antecedent. Consider these sentences.

Wrong: The author who understands grammar will be proud of their finished product.

Correct: The author who understands grammar will be proud of his or her finished product.

"The author" is singular and must have a singular pronoun. Yes, it is tedious to have to write "his or her" in that sentence, but "their" does not agree with "the author," which is singular. Or, you can rewrite the sentence.

Correct: *Authors* who understand grammar will be proud of *their* finished product.

Wrong: The writer who isn't careful will soon discover they have made a mistake.

Wrong: She is also a member of the XYZ Bar Association and active with their Young Lawyers' Division.

Note: This particular Bar Association's website has the Division as a) the Young Lawyer's Division, b) the Young Lawyers' Division, and c) the Young Lawyers Division. Sloppy.

Wrong: The group is writing their own story.

Correct: The group is writing its own story.

Wrong: In a criminal case, the defendant is subject to losing their *freedom* as opposed to property lost in a civil case.

When two singular antecedents are joined by *and*, generally they will take a plural pronoun; when two singular antecedents are joined by *or* or *nor*, they take a singular pronoun.

Liz and Rich found their dream home.

Neither Bob nor Rich ever found his true love.

(You will get tripped up in a sentence like the one above if you are talking about a man and a woman, since pronouns have to agree in gender, as well as singular/plural. It's best to rewrite on those occasions.)

Like the noun-verb agreement rule earlier, if two antecedents are joined by *or* or *nor*, and one is singular and the other plural, the pronoun generally agrees with the nearest antecedent, like so:

Neither her book nor her short stories have lost their appeal.

Either cookies or cake has its advantages as a dessert.

**The so-called singular "they."**

Don't get me started. When writer is so sloppy that he or she refers to an individual as a "they," we have a problem. A big one. I'm not wading into gender politics, but I will say that good writing is precise. Until a gender neutral singular pronoun is created, one that is easy to spell, easy to pronounce, and makes sense, count me out about using "they" to refer to an individual. Not gonna happen. It might be easy, but it sure is sloppy.

Sloppy writing = muddy thinking. Be precise.

**Gender "neutralizing" your writing.**

Don't go there. Always tend towards precision.

The *men* who have been president.

The *men* who have landed on the moon.

The pregnant *women* who are affected by the law.

The *men* I have dated.

## Let's test your knowledge!

Take a look at these sentences, which are all right off the internet. What's wrong? (Answers follow.)

1. You are provided with the speaker's contact information up front, so that you can screen them personally, before signing any contracts.

2. He is known for a engaging and entertaining style.

3. Written in zippy, conversational prose, this is a must-have for anyone interested in advancing themselves personally and professionally.

4. Your featured guest will probably already have their own materials.

5. We recognize our fulfillment services are an extension of your brand and tied to the impression your customer gets when they receive packages we fulfill on your behalf.

6. When your friend activates a Square account through your link, they can process up to $1,000 in credit card sales for free.

7. Our in-house resources consists of dedicated professionals who, prior to joining Sun Capital, spent their careers operating businesses.

8. To view the depth and expertise of each team member, click their photo.

9. Each of the company's leaders tell a personal story of applying knowledge from working within the for-profit world with expertise learned in aiding foundations and non-profits.

10. "The fact is," he says, "none of us knows what the catastrophically injured claimant endures, even when the claim is 100% their fault."

11. We are a great organization built on the strength of its guiding principles.

12. At Investopedia, we empower each individual to succeed, communicate their ideas, and take action.

13. The separation of church and state is a beautiful tenant that encourages personal religious freedom and the prevention of religion imposed by the state.

**Answers.**

1. "The speaker's" is singular, but "them" is plural.

Correct: You are provided with the speakers' contact information up front, so that you can screen them personally, before signing any contracts.

Correct: You are provided with the speaker's contact information up front, so that you can screen him or her personally, before signing a contract.

Better: You are provided with each speaker's contact information up front, so that you can screen him or her personally, before signing a contract.

2. Wrong article. You can't put "a" in front of a word that starts with an "e" sound. You've got to use *an*.

Correct: He is known for an engaging and entertaining style.

Better: He is known for his engaging and entertaining style.

3. "Anyone" is singular; "themselves" is not.

Correct: Written in zippy, conversational prose, this is a must-have for anyone interested in advancing him- or herself personally and professionally.

Better: Written in zippy, conversational prose, this book is a must-have for everyone interested in advancing him- or herself, personally and professionally.

Even better: Written in zippy, conversational prose, [book title here] is a must-have for everyone interested in advancing him- or herself, both personally *and* professionally.

4. Your featured guest [singular] will probably already have their [plural] own materials.

Correct: Your featured guests will probably already have their own materials.

Correct: Your featured guest will probably already have his or her own materials.

5. "Customer" is singular; "they" is plural. (Otherwise, what a mouthful!)

Correct: We recognize our fulfillment services are an extension of your brand and tied to the impression your customers get when they receive packages we fulfill on your behalf.

6. "Friend" is singular; "they" is plural.

Correct: When your friends activate a Square account through your link, they can process up to $1,000 in credit card sales for free.

7. "Resources" is plural; "consists" is singular.

Correct: Our in-house resources consist of dedicated professionals who, prior to joining Sun Capital, spent their careers operating businesses.

8. "Member" is singular; "their" is plural. I would also suggest adding "on" to "click." To be honest, I'm not crazy about this sentence, however it is written.

Correct: To view the depth and expertise of each team member, click on his or her photo.

A little better: To understand more fully the depth and expertise of each team member, click on his or her photo.

A little better: To read more about each team member, click on his or her photo.

9. There are a couple of problems with this sentence. First off, "each" is singular, so "tell" should be "tells." Second, "nonprofits" has no hyphen.

Correct: Each of the company's leaders tells a personal story of applying knowledge from working within the for-profit world with expertise learned in aiding foundations and nonprofits.

10. "Claimant" is singular; "their" is plural.

Better: The fact is," he says, "none of us knows what the catastrophically injured claimant endures, even when the claim is 100% that person's fault."

11. The subject in this sentence is "we," not "organization," so the sentence should read, "We are a great organization, built on the strength of our guiding principles."

12. "Individual" is singular; "their" is plural.

13. Ooops! It's *tenet*, not *tenant*.

## Verbs.

A *verb* is a word (or a group of words) that defines an activity, asserts something, or indicates a state of being. A verb is used when making a statement, asking a question, or giving a command. Verbs change tense to show the *when* of a sentence. Without a verb no group of words is grammatically a complete sentence.

Example: A flood of lurid light poured into Miss Mapp's mind.

A verb may consist of a single word or a group of words. The group is often referred to as a *verb phrase*, and is made up of the verb plus auxiliary words such as *are, am, about to, be, been, began to, can, could, does, did, going to, had, had to, has, has to, have, have to, is, may, might, must, ought to, shall, should, was, were,* and *will.*

The words in a verb phrase do not have to be sequential.

Example: But what did a true Tillingite want with a butler and a motor car?

At a minimum, a complete sentence contains a verb and its subject.

Example: Miss Mapp looked much surprised.

In order to find the subject of a sentence, ask yourself "Who or what?" in connection with the verb. In the previous example, who or what "looked"? Answer: Miss Mapp looked.

Example: I drove the Porsche 911 Turbo S Cabriolet like a maniac.

Finding the object of the verb is simple: ask yourself who or what was affected by the verb. So, what did I drive? Answer: the Porsche.

Example: Elizabeth was now in possession of what she wanted to know.

Question: What did Elizabeth possess?

Answer: What she wanted to know.

Sometimes a verb such as *bring, buy, give, lend, offer, send, sell,* and *take* may have both a direct and an indirect object. To find the indirect object, ask yourself: To whom or for whom was the activity done?

Example: With the enormous profits from her book sales, Liz bought herself a brand new Porsche 911 Turbo S Cabriolet in Amethyst Metallic.

Subject: Liz

Verb: bought

Object: a Porsche

Indirect object: herself

Even though most of us have access to the spell-check feature of our word processors, here's a handy trick to spelling the *–ing* and *–ed* tenses of many verbs: If the first syllable is accented, then don't double the last consonant (barrel/barreled, cancel/canceled, visit/visiting); if a second or subsequent syllable is accented, then double the last consonant, as in these words: admit/admitting, begin/beginning, compel/compelling, permit/permitting, occur/occurring. Exceptions include verbs that end in "h," "w," "x," and "y." Who knew?!

## Intransitive and transitive verbs.

There are two types of verbs: *intransitive* verbs and *transitive* verbs.

An intransitive verb does not need an object: He ran.

Examples of intransitive verbs: *arrive, reoccur, die, happen.*

A transitive verb needs an object: She bought the book.

Examples of transitive verbs: *advocate, afflict, buy, clean, hit, kick, kill, inflict, load, offer, paint, pay, play, read, refuse, teach, want,* and *write.*

The test to show whether a verb is transitive or intransitive is that an intransitive verb cannot have a passive form.

Active: I died. Not: I was died.

The verb *kill,* on the other hand, is transitive, and you know that because it has a passive form.

Active: I killed it. Passive: It was killed by me.

Some verbs can be both transitive and intransitive. Examples: *admit, attack, clash, divide, eat, float, fly, go, match, paint, run, sell.*

## Subjunctive use of the verb *to be.*

The subjunctive tense happens when the "mood" of a verb expresses hope or a wish about something that isn't true, something that is hypothetical or, as Philip B. Corbett, editing guru at *The New York Times,* puts it nicely: a "contrary-to-fact condition." Oftentimes, a sentence calling for the subjunctive describes a possible future action and starts with *if*: If *this*, then *that* could happen or would happen.

When using the subjunctive form of the verb *to be*, instead of saying "If I was," you'd write "If I were..."

Example: "I think I shall go out for my drive, Peppino," she said, "though if I were you I would nurse my cold and get it all right before Saturday when we go to Adele's."

Often, the subjunctive mood seems to strike people while they are singing, so you hear Johnny Cash asking "If I were a carpenter..." and Tevye, in *Fiddler on a Roof*, wondering what would happen "If I were a rich man...."

However, if there's a reasonable likelihood that what you are writing about is true or has happened, you'd write *was* (which is called the "indicative" mood).

Not to belabor the point, but watch out for the subjunctive tense and conjugate accordingly.

### Split infinitives.

A "split infinitive" is an adverb or an adverb phrase that comes between the "marker" *to* and the verb.

Example: I need to really learn some Italian phrases before I go there.

In this example, the adverb *really* "splits" the verb *learn* and its marker *to*.

Winston Churchill hated split infinitives, but they pass unremarked in modern-day writing and conversation.

## Part 2: Punctuation and grammar.

### "A" vs. An.

Remember, the decision to use "a" or *an* depends on the *sound* that the following word begins with. So....

"a" + some singular noun beginning with a consonant: *a* book, *a* chocolate bar

*an* + some singular nouns beginning with a vowel: *an* editor, *an* ice cream cone, *an* Italian beach, *an* elegy *an* + many letters of the alphabet when used as single letters or as part of an abbreviation (e.g., an "a," an "s," and an "f," *an* MD, *an* MBA, *an* NFL player, *an* SBA loan, *an* NYSE-listed stock).

Those exceptions happen because some individual letters—whether or not they are vowels—start with a vowel sound: "s" is pronounced *ess*, "m" is pronounced *em*, and so on.

Using an abbreviation or acronym can make a difference.

"a" Small Business Administration loan versus *an* SBA loan

"a" New York Stock Exchange stock versus *an* NYSE stock

"a" + singular noun beginning with vowel with a consonant sound: *a* university ("university" begins with a consonant "y" sound, so "a" is used), *a* Utah tourist, *a* universal truth, *a* European plan, *a* once-over, *a* eulogy, *a* euphemism, *a* one-on-one

*an* + nouns starting with silent "h": *an* hour late, *an* honest mistake, *an* honorable discharge, *an* heirloom tomato

"a" + nouns starting with a pronounced "h": *a* handsome horse, *a* horror film, *a* hard day's work

Note: Interestingly, some people *say* "an historic event," but they *write* "a historic event." Try it:

*An* historical event is worth remembering.

*A* historical event is worth remembering.

These rules also apply with acronyms.

Example: *An* AFL-CIO membership was necessary for the job.

Example: *A* TSA agent asked me where I was going.

## Abbreviations and acronyms.

An abbreviation is a shortening of a word or phrase, while an acronym is a word (or letters pronounced individually) created by the letters or parts of the words of a phrase.

Note: If you are looking for the right way to shorten a word or phrase, in the sense of a contraction (e.g., ma'am, lookin', etc.), please review the section about apostrophes.

**Use abbreviations with care.**

In formal writing, you should avoid abbreviations.

Example: the Florida Supreme Court, not the FL Supreme Court.

If you write about the Florida Supreme Court and the United States Supreme Court, be sure to clarify to which you are referring. In fact, always spell out "United States" when United States is used as a noun: the Supreme Court of the United States. When "United States" is used as an adjective in informal writing, US is acceptable, but *AP* says to use U.S. Be consistent.

Given this guideline, the use below would be incorrect, and especially so since this seems to be more formal writing than not:

In my dissertation, I targeted English-speaking adult visitors to natural history museums, science centers, and zoos in the US.

Similarly, it is generally more acceptable to spell out words like Saint, Fort, Mount, and so on, as opposed to abbreviating.

Examples:

Fort Myers, Mount Saint Mary, Port Saint Joe

The first time you use a lengthy name that you plan to shorten, use the name and follow by either the abbreviation in parenthesis or a phrase such as "commonly known as," followed by the acronym.

Examples:

The jobs provided by the Tennessee Valley Authority (TVA) were an important part of our country's recovery.

The jobs provided by the Tennessee Valley Authority (commonly known as the TVA) were an important part of our country's recovery.

The jobs provided by the Tennessee Valley Authority, commonly known as the TVA, were an important part of our country's recovery.

If you feel that your readers might forget what the acronym stands for, refresh their memories from time to time and spell everything out.

Beware industry-specific or new acronyms that might not be well known outside your specialty. Never assume that your readers will know what you are talking about; for example, here's an acronym I saw for the first time today: Europe, Middle East & Africa (EMEA).

An acronym can be a handy mnemonic (memory aid). A great example is PEWSAGL, which is an especially helpful way to remember the seven deadly sins (and in descending order, too!): P-ride, E-nvy, W-rath, S-loth, A-nger, G-luttony, and L-ust.

Another good acronym to assist in remembering the names of America's Great Lakes is HOMES: Huron, Ontario, Michigan, Erie, and Superior.

Interestingly, according to *The New York Times*, when an acronym is used as a proper name and is longer than four letters, only the first letter is capitalized: Unicef, for example; though it seems that this rule exists only because of that whole caps-equals-shouting thing on the internet. However, it is more polite (not to mention accurate) to use the case preferred by the owner of a trademarked acronym (C-SPAN, NASCAR) than to worry overmuch about a little noisy online chatter. When in doubt, look it up.

**If an acronym is so commonly used that it has become standard, do not use periods between the letters.**

Examples: the NAACP, not the N.A.A.C.P; the FBI, not the F.B.I; the KKK, not the K.K.K.

Plus, ASAP, FYI, ESP, CIA, EST, FDA, LSD, NHL, RSVP, NCAA, USA, NFL, PGA, UFO, URL, DUI, BYOB, BLT, FAQ, SOS, ACC, ISBN, IRS, RIP, snafu, mph, mpg, etc.

However, here are two exceptions, according to *The New York Times*: G.I. Bill and the C.D.C.

Here are two more: B.C., meaning "before Christ," and A.D., for anno Domini (in the year of the Lord).

According to some style manuals, the "no period" policy also extends to academic and professional titles, with very few exceptions. Please see the "Titles and honorifics" section for more details.

Examples: MD, JD, MBA, BA, BS, DDS, PhD, JP, RN, MP, etc.

If you do choose to use periods, be consistent.

When writing a person's name, followed by his or her academic title, enclose the title with commas.

Example: Elizabeth H. Coursen, BA, wrote this book.

Compass points require no periods: NE, NW, SSW, S, N, and so on.

If a character's nickname is a single letter, some authors choose not to use a period after the letter. This decision, however, is up to you; so, if you feel more comfortable with the period after the end of a single-letter nickname, use it, but make sure you are consistent. I prefer the period after a single letter myself.

Examples:

Fred watched as Mr. C walked up the stairs.

"C'mon, Mr. C, let's hurry," he called.

Some common expressions have been abbreviated and their meaning is generally understood: aka, fka, swf. In legal documents, you will often see certain abbreviations with slashes between the letters: a/k/a, f/k/a. Make sure you are consistent in your usage throughout.

**Abbreviated dimensions.**

When you abbreviate dimensions, typically no period follows the term; the abbreviations for *inch* and *foot* are exceptions.

Examples:

centimeter: cm
pound: lb
inch: in.

**The use of abbreviations is also permitted in legal names.**

Example: WaMu. However, even though this is a trademarked name that is part of a larger entity, for clarity's sake you may decide to write Washington Mutual Bank (or, if necessary, Washington Mutual Bank, FA) instead.

Example: L.L. Bean (Not too many people know that the L. L. stood for Leon Leonwood.)

Always strive for accuracy: visit official corporate websites and double-check.

**Common Latin abbreviations.**

Common Latin abbreviations include etc., et al., e.g., and c.v., which means *curriculum vitae*. However, "c.v." seems to be in a certain amount of flux, since some style manuals also use CV or cv. It would seem that the version with the periods would be more consistent with other common Latin-phrase abbreviations, which all have at least one accompanying period.

"Versus" is a Latin word which, despite its brevity, has spawned not one but two abbreviations: "v." and "vs." Both abbreviations use a period. The "v." abbreviation is commonly used in lawsuits (*Coursen v. Watrous*), and the "vs." is used in sports events and comparisons (Georgia Tech vs. Georgia).

**Plural forms of abbreviations and acronyms.**

To create a plural of an abbreviation or acronym, add a lowercase "s," as in IRAs, MDs, URLs, CEOs, BAs, FAQs, etc.

The plural of an abbreviation with periods can be formed by adding an apostrophe + "s": M.D.'s, I.P.O.'s, and so on. The problem with this form of plural is that it is identical to the possessive, and so could cause confusion; for clarity's sake, you might want to forgo the periods and the apostrophe, because, as it turns out, the apostrophe continues to confuse.

Take a look at this sentence, and you'll see what I mean:

These appeals all concern the activities of the Florida Department of Health and Rehabilitative Services (HRS) with regard to the granting of CON's to applicants to operate as home health care agencies.

## Accents and symbols.

Many foreign words require a special accent to be spelled properly. Some don't, though, because they've become commonly accepted here: rôle, for example, has become role. However, one accent mark can make a big difference! Consider: resume (to continue) vs. résumé (a list of accomplishments), and pécher (to sin) vs. pêcher (to fish). When in doubt, consult a dictionary.

To create these accents and symbols in Word, turn on the Number Lock on your computer keyboard (it's over to the far right, just above the number keys), "mouse-over" the letter and, while holding down the ALT key, type these numbers on the number key to the far right. When you "undo" the mouse-over, the appropriate accent/symbol should appear. Note: you use a different number to form a capital letter's accent.

For all you good people using a Mac, I'm sorry to say I would suggest you turn to our friend Google. When I did, I couldn't make heads or tails of the entries. I hope you have better luck.

**FRENCH**

à (0224) À (0192) â (0226) Â (0194)

æ (145 or 0230) Æ (0198)

ç (0231) Ç (0199)

é (0233) É (0201) è (0232) È (0200)

ê (0234) Ê (0202) ë (0235) Ë (0203)

î (0238) Î (0206) ï (0239) Ï (0207)

œ(0156) Œ (0140)

ô (0244) Ô (0212)

ù (0249) Ù (0217) û (0251) Û (0219)

**GERMAN/SCANDINAVIAN**

ä (0228) Ä (0196) å (0229) Å (0197)

æ (145 or 0230) Æ (0198)

ë (0235) Ë (0203)

ð (0240) Đ (0208) ö (0246) Ö (0214)

ø (0248) Ø (0216)

ß (0223)

þ (0254) Þ (0222)

ü (0252) Ü (0220)

ÿ (0255) Ÿ (0159)

**ITALIAN**

à (0224) À (0192)

è (0232) È (0200)

ì (0236) Ì (0204)

ò (0242) Ò (0210)

ù (0249) Ù (0217)

**SPANISH**

á (0225) Á (0193)

é (0233) É (0201)

í (0237) Í (0205)

ñ (0241) Ñ (0209)

ó (0243) Ó (0211)

ú (0250) Ú (0218) ü (0252) Ü (0220)

**PORTUGUESE**

ã (0227) Ã (0195)

ç (0231) Ç (0199)

**Using your keyboard to create symbols.**

Bullet ( • ) is Alt 0 1 4 9

Copyright (©) is Alt 0 1 6 9

Ellipsis (…) is Alt 0 1 3 3

"EM" Dash ( — ) is Alt 0 1 5 1

"EN" Dash ( – ) is Alt 0 1 5 0

Paragraph (Pilcrow) ( ¶ ) is Alt 0 1 8 2

Registered ( ® ) is Alt 0 1 7 4

Trademark ( ™ ) is Alt 0 1 5 3

Degree ( ° ) Alt 0 1 7 6

Pound ( £ ) is Alt 0 1 6 3

Euro ( € ) is Alt 0 1 2 8

Cents ( ¢ ) is Alt 0 1 6 2

One-half (½) is Alt 0 1 8 9

« is Alt 0 1 7 1

» is Alt 0 1 8 7

## Apostrophes.

Note: some fonts have "directional" or "smart" apostrophes (apostrophes that face one way or another), while other fonts have straight up-and-down apostrophes. If you use a font with directional apostrophes (like this one, which is called "Bookman Old Style"), watch the direction of your apostrophes. Sometimes when using Microsoft Word you will have to play around with an apostrophe to make it face the right way. Also, make sure your apostrophe and your singular quotation mark look identical; in other words, don't mix directional quotation marks with nondirectional apostrophes. It looks sloppy.

**The apostrophe has four uses:**

- to form possessives of nouns (see the Possessive section for that use)
- to show the omission of letters or numbers
- in a contraction
- to indicate plurals of single letters, single numbers, and acronyms with periods

**Apostrophes show the omission of letters and numbers.**

When indicating an omission of letters or numbers, the apostrophe faces "out" when the first portion of a word is not there.

Example: A whole 'nuther ballgame.

If the missing portion of the word is at the end, the apostrophe faces "in," as in "singin' in the rain."

From time to time, you'll need an apostrophe before and after the abbreviated word.

Example: rock 'n' roll.

You may have to play with your word processor to achieve that effect.

Sometimes, but not often, an apostrophe is combined with a hyphen, like this: will-o'-the-wisp, jack-o'-lantern.

Use an apostrophe before figures expressing a decade or a year if numerals are left out: the '90s, '72.

Note: Use the letter "s" but not an apostrophe after the figures when expressing decades or centuries, e.g., the 1900s.

**Apostrophes are used in contractions.**

A contraction is a word which is formed when two words are joined. The apostrophe indicates this joining. Contractions are common in informal writing and in dialog, especially when illustrating a regional dialect. Often, but not always, you will place an apostrophe where the joining occurs. Here are some examples:

don't = do not; I'm = I am

she'll = she will; who's = who is

shouldn't = should not; didn't = did not

could've = could have (NOT "could of"!)

Be careful. Sometimes an author will contract *is* and couple it with a noun, as in "First thing's first." While this type of contraction can be effective in dialog, do not use it in formal writing; it is not a standard use and can be confusing to your readers.

Be even more careful. If you do decide to couple *is* with a noun or pronoun, be sure that *is* is the correct verb. Take a look at this sentence, which I found on a "professional" copy editor's blog:

If you're having trouble hitting the mark, here's three tips to help you write effective persuasive copy while still keeping the reader engaged.

The contraction is *here's*, which means *here is*. However, here is what? Here *is* three things? Oh, no. Here *are* three things. There's no such thing as a contraction of *here are*. And, frankly, there is a comma needed between *effective* and *persuasive*. The sentence would have to read as follows to be correct:

If you're having trouble hitting the mark, here are three tips to help you write effective, persuasive copy while still keeping the reader engaged.

But that is really not correct in formal writing. I would not suggest using a contraction for "here + are" unless you are writing dialog.

This is not standard, either:

We've not recently heard from you and would like to schedule some time to discuss your book and publishing goals in more detail.

More acceptable would be "We haven't heard from you recently..."

**Very important point:** *That's* is either the contraction of *that is* or *that has*, but it *is not* the possessive of *that*. The possessive of *that* is *whose*.

**Apostrophes are often used to create "slangy" dialog.**

Examples:

"C'mon," he replied skeptically.

"Right, m'boy," she answered. "C'mere."

"The ground was good 'n' hard."

"Yes, ma'am."

"Like Hollywood, y'know?"

Note: a use like this is different from a deliberately misspelled or incorrect word, like *coulda* or *ain't*.

**An apostrophe + "s" is used to form the plural of single letters.**

Apostrophes are used to form plurals of both upper- and lowercase single letters: here the rule appears to be more typographical, for clarity, than grammatical, e.g., "three ts" (wrong) versus "three T's" (correct). To form the plural of a single letter, use an apostrophe + an "s" after the letter: P's and Q's, three R's. For clarity, I suggest using capitals in this situation.

The plural of two or more capital letters is formed by adding a lowercase "s": MBAs, CPAs, LSATs.

**Tricky possessives: *its* and *whose*.**

Watch your use of *its* and *whose*, and double-check your final draft to make sure you haven't made an inadvertent error.

This is one of the—if not *the*—most common mistakes in the English language:

It's = it is

"Its" is the possessive of "it."

Wrong: The library made it's decision.

Correct: The library made its decision.

Who's = who is

"Whose" is the possessive of "who" and "that."

Wrong: As a mother who's mentally ill son has been transported by law officers, it made me sick.

Correct: As a mother whose mentally ill son has been transported by law officers, it made me sick.

Mistakenly using *it's* for *its* and vice versa is particularly insidious and will make you look like an idiot. I suggest doing a document "search" for *its* and *it's* right before you hit the "print" button.

**When you *don't* need an apostrophe.**

You certainly don't use an apostrophe to form the plural of words or anything other than single-digit numbers or single letters. Alas, it is plain that not everyone knows this rule:

Be sure to scroll down for more photo's.

Ask Spotlight Graphics' to recommend the best finishing option for your project.

There is no need for an apostrophe to indicate the plural form of capitalized letters, numbers, figures, and symbols.

Example: two '98 Titanium Lamborghini Diablo Roadster VTs with black interiors and rear spoilers

Used in a sentence: If I had my way, I'd own two identical 1998 Lamborghini Diablo Roadster VTs: one to drive while the other is in the shop!

Examples:

too many *s = too many asterisks

the 1960s = years in the decade from 1960 through 1969

Don't use apostrophes for personal pronouns, the relative pronoun *who*, or for plural nouns.

Apostrophes should not be used with possessive pronouns—*his, her, its, my, yours*—because possessive pronouns already show possession—they don't need an apostrophe. (Try to pronounce yours' or yours's and you'll see what I mean.)

Wrong: her' book

Correct: her book

However, indefinite pronouns, such as *one, someone, no one, anyone, other*, and *anybody* can be made possessive. Here are a couple of examples:

Correct: someone's book

Correct: anyone's book

Be careful. Watch your use of apostrophes. Consider this sentence:

The canal's no longer in use, but the animated trading goes on.

This apostrophe could be momentarily confusing: the canal's *what* is no longer in use? After repeated reading it becomes clear that the author is using this apostrophe as a contraction for "The canal is": not a standard use, but (marginally) acceptable.

However, consider the sentence that follows "the canal" sentence:

The market's lower level is dominated by produce, flower, and meat vendors.

So, this paragraph started with these two sentences:

The canal's no longer in use, but the animated trading goes on. The market's lower level is dominated by produce, flower, and meat vendors.

In successive sentences we have subject + apostrophe, but with different purposes: the first sentence, when the apostrophe is used in its contraction role (however confusing), and the second sentence, when the apostrophe was used to create a possessive. If the first apostrophe was confusing, the use of the second one made it worse.

Here is another good example of a writer who did not know (or care) to use apostrophes correctly. In the sentence that follows, we need an apostrophe for the contraction of "what" and "is," and we need an apostrophe to create the plural possessive of "customer."

We build custom marketing plans and convert those plans into action, constantly measuring whats working to achieve our customers goals.

Let me ask you: How much confidence does that sentence give you about the care and attention this company will bring to your marketing plan? Shoot, this is *seriously* sloppy writing!

**Apostrophe...not!**

BE CAREFUL. Sometimes something that looks like an apostrophe isn't. I'm referring to measurements, in inches and feet. Those are called prime marks: inches is a single “prime" mark ('), and feet is represented by a “double prime” mark (''):

He jumped 5' 2'' as a 13-year-old athlete.

The prime marks above are one single quote after the 5, and two single quotes after the 2. There was no other way I could figure out how to create the nondirectional prime marks.

## Appositives.

An appositive is a word or phrase that adds explanatory or clarifying information to the noun or noun phrase that precedes it. Put another way, an appositive is a word or phrase that “stands in” for another. So, in the sentence: “Sarasota, the prettiest place in the world, is home to the world’s most beautiful beach,” the phrase “the prettiest place in the world” is the appositive.

That sentence could also be written: “The prettiest place in the world, Sarasota, is home to the world’s most beautiful beach,” which would make “Sarasota” the appositive.

Typically, the information given by the appositive is nonrestrictive, that is, it is not necessary to the sentence. A singular nonrestrictive appositive is set off by commas.

Example:

I adopted Grace, my lab-chow mix, from the pound—she was scheduled to be put down the next day.

Sometimes, though, an appositive gives *necessary* information. A restrictive appositive is not set off by commas.

Examples:

The Indian Chief Crazy Horse was among the slain.

An Indian Chief, Crazy Horse, was among the slain.

Crazy Horse, an Indian Chief, was among the slain.

Crazy Horse was among the slain.

Once you've said "the," what follows is necessary and not set off by commas. If, however, you'd said "a," or "an," as in "An Indian Chief, Crazy Horse," was among those slain," then the name of the particular Indian Chief is not necessary.

When punctuating a sentence with a compound appositive, use dashes, not commas, to make sure your readers understand what you are saying.

Consider this sentence:

My cousins, Tina, Jeff, and Kim, arrived at the party late.

What you are trying to say is that your cousins, whose names are Tina, Jeff, and Kim, arrived late. If so, then "Tina, Jeff, and Kim" is the compound appositive. That might be what you meant, but that's not what you said. Why aren't we sure? Because, the way the sentence is written, we don't know if Tina, Jeff, and Kim are the cousins or are party-goers who also arrived "late" with your cousins. In fact, the way it's written, it looks as though "Tina, Jeff, and Kim" *and* your cousins arrived late.

However, when the sentence is punctuated with dashes, the meaning becomes clear:

My cousins—Tina, Jeff, and Kim—arrived at the party late.

## Brackets.

Brackets are used to indicate that you are adding or omitting words in someone else's original text. If you add a word or words to someone else's work, use brackets to indicate which words are yours. If you incorporate the beginning of a sentence written by someone else into your work, use brackets to indicate the change from uppercase to lowercase.

Example: In the glow of forgiveness, Major Benjy decided that "[r]equests for the present were certainly commands, and two minutes later they set forth."

Another time to use brackets is when you are quoting someone else's work with a misspelled word or other mistake in the material. If this happens, write "sic" inside brackets: [sic]. This alerts your reader that a) there is a mistake of some sort, and b) it isn't yours.

## Capitalization.

There is way too much capitalization going on! Inappropriate capitalization sounds pretentious. Take a look at this sentence:

They envisioned a Trial Firm whose lawyers had outstanding litigation and courtroom skills, were respected by the bench and bar, and, importantly, were dedicated to client service.

A "Trial Firm"? Please. Give me a break.

Always capitalize proper names and the names of rivers, mountain ranges, streets, and locations.

Example: Philippi Creek runs under Webber Street.

However, when a word or phrase originally derived from a proper name has assumed a more general usage, do not capitalize the proper name.

Examples: french fry, venetian blinds, vulcanize, satanic

When common nouns are plural, referring to two or more places or things, do not capitalize them.

Examples:

I have sailed on both the Pacific and Atlantic oceans.

We invited representatives from both the Republican and Democratic parties.

Chapter 1. Punctuation and Grammar.

When referring to a title or headline, always capitalize the first word and all other words except "a," *an, and, as, at, but, by, for, from, if, in, its, of, on, or, the, this, to, with,* and *without,* unless they follow a colon or unless it's the font "style."

Example: *Self-Editing for the Successful Pre-Law Student: You Need this Book!*

Sometimes, but not always, the second word of a hyphenated word in a title is not capitalized; exceptions would be if the second word is a noun, a proper adjective, or if it is equal in importance to the first word.

Do not capitalize the words north, south, northeast, etc., when they indicate direction; North, South, West, etc., are capitalized when they indicate geographical regions: the North, the West, the Southeast, the Western frontier, the Deep South, and so on. Words and phrases such as the Windy City, Motor City, Big Apple, Sunshine State, Gold Coast, Mid Atlantic, Silicon Valley, Dixie, Gulf Coast, Cotton Belt, Rust Belt, Deep South, Northern Hemisphere, Mason Dixon Line, Outer Banks, Middle East, and Vacationland are capitalized.

Periods of time are also capitalized: Bronze Age, Stone Age, Space Age, etc. Exceptions: ice age (because there was more than one), the twentieth century.

Capitalize the names of Greek and Roman gods (Venus, Zeus, Thor), as well as entities that aren't real but have become proper names (Big Brother, Mother Nature).

The seasons (fall, winter, spring, summer) are typically not capitalized. An exception, for example, would be Fall 2015.

I would capitalize branches of the U.S. military service: Army, Air Force, Navy, Marines, Coast Guard, both as names and as adjectives, except for *naval,* when used as an adjective, as in naval regulations and naval attaché.

However, my idol when it comes to militaristic writing, Tom Clancy, capitalizes references to the military services only when they are preceded by "U.S." Take a look at these sentences and sentence fragments from *The Hunt for Red October*:

The pilots were up twice a day or more, exercising with their U.S. Air Force and Navy counterparts.

That's an expression we use in the navy.

Once upon a time I was a lieutenant in the marines...

The navy had succeeded...

The air force had sent down a VCV-135 transport...

...expressing the professional admiration of the U.S. Air Force...

...smiling U. S. Navy doctors...

See the "Titles and honorifics" section for rules about when to capitalize names, academic degrees, positions, etc.

Use common sense. Most of the time, for clarity's sake, capitalize words or phrases that mean something more than they do as individual words or phrases. As an example, when using the phrase "plan b" to indicate an alternate (and second choice) course of action, you could write plan b, plan B, or Plan B. All of these choices would be correct. However, of the options, Plan B shows exactly what you mean to convey without forcing your reader to hesitate, go back, and figure out what you meant, which would be necessary if either of the other two options was used. Besides, there is something inelegant about leaving a lowercase letter other than "a" dangling in the middle of a sentence.

Similarly, if you refer to a book called *The Pocket Guide to Brunswick, Maine, with Two Maps* repeatedly throughout your work and from time to time you shorten the title to *The Pocket Guide*, it makes no sense not to capitalize (and italicize!) The Pocket Guide, because, otherwise, the pocket guide just blends right into the text and disappears.

## Let's test your knowledge!

What's wrong with these sentences? (Answers follow.)

1. We help to connect certified pet therapy volunteer teams with area nursing homes, assisted living facilities, social service agencies, schools and libraries throughout the Sarasota and Manatee Counties.

2. In the Fall of 1951, Donald Evans lost his dog.

3. She left USF to form her own Consulting Company focused on Resiliency based in Innate Health.

4. Prior to this, she worked for a national firm as an audit manager for large public entities including the City of Chicago, O'Hare and Midway Airports, the Chicago Housing Authority, the Chicago Transit Authority and the Philadelphia Housing Authority.

5. Furthermore, CPA's are sought after for their expertise.

6. For those who aspire to the Audit world, addressing company Boards is a required practice.

7. Joyce has over 20 years experience in the enterprise applications market.

8. John's ideas about decisions are sure to inspire, inform, and educate and will elevate your level of performance everyday!

9. Don your most elegantly-electric formal attire, mysterious masque and sense of adventure at the historic opera house.

10. Using our software, they've sent over 7,000 emails on behalf of the sales team—drastically increasing sales reps efficiency.

11. The cleaning crew is supposed to be restricted to the zoo's restrooms and gift shop and are not allowed in animal enclosures.

12. When clerk did not object to case against it being brought it small claims, court had jurisdiction under small claims rules to entertain plaintiff's claims that it should be refunded a $50 reopen fee paid in another case. *Burke v. Esposito*, 1.5 Fla. L. Weekly Supp. 205 (6th Cir. Ct. 2007) (appellate capacity).

13. After seeing the assigned lector's reading for the first time on Saturday night, Liz felt a twinge of jealousy that surprised her. How she wished she were reading the passage. What wonderful drama! She read it five or six

times and felt, for the first time ever, like she wanted to raise her hands like a Baptist. She decided to put her hat in the ring for the *next* year c, second Sunday after Easter, reading from the Revelation to John. Let someone else read on Easter!

**Answers.**

1. “Counties” should not be capitalized; it’s that plural-of-the-common-noun rule.

2. Don’t capitalize a season.

3. Why, pray, is “Consulting Company” capitalized? And what in the world is “Resiliency based in Innate Health”? Is it a thing? If so, it’s a proper noun phrase and the capitalization is proper. However, I’ve got $50 that says it isn’t.

4. At a minimum, “airports” should not be capitalized, and you definitely want a comma between those last two items.

Correct: Prior to this, she worked for a national firm as an audit manager for large public entities, including the City of Chicago, O’Hare and Midway airports, the Chicago Housing Authority, the Chicago Transit Authority, and the Philadelphia Housing Authority.

5. When an abbreviation has no periods, it is best to form the plural by adding an “s,” not an apostrophe + “s.”

6. Neither “audit” nor “boards” should have been capitalized.

7. “Years” is possessive here, and so needs an apostrophe: Joyce has over 20 years’ experience in the enterprise applications market.

8. *Inform* and *educate* are so close in meaning that using one is enough. There will need to be a comma before *and* in the *and will* phrase. Plus, it’s every day, not everyday. The exclamation mark kind of adds insult to injury. Here’s a slightly better version of this sentence: John’s ideas about decisions are sure to inspire, inform, and improve your level of performance every day.

9. “Masque” is not the preferred spelling; it’s “mask.” Plus, you really do need that serial comma between the last two items in this list.

10. “Sales reps” definitely needs to be possessive: sales reps’. Also, the word “drastic” has a negative connotation, meaning severe, sharp, painful:

plastic surgery can be drastic, layoffs can be drastic, drastic measures are not good. "Dramatically" would have been much better.

11. *Crew* is a collective noun, and so is singular. "Are" should be "is."

12. Pronoun confusion: "it" refers to two different things here, which makes this confusing to the reader. However, the importance of *accurate typing skills* is the point of including this content, found on page 6 of *Florida Small Claims Rules Annotated* (2020-2021 edition). Don't see the problem? Read it again! Read it until you *see* it.

13. Doesn't "Year C" blend in to the rest of the text? If capitalizing a concept will help a reader to more quickly and accurately understand your message, then you have my permission to capitalize phrases like Year C, Plan B, Door Number Three and so on and give them proper noun status.

## Colons.

A colon separates two parts of a sentence when the first part creates a sense of anticipation about the content of the second part.

Here's an easy way to think of a colon: imagine yourself pointing to a burglar hiding in the bushes and shouting to the police, "He's here! He's here!" That's the role of the colon. Use the colon as an arrow, pointing to what comes next in the sentence.

Before you use a colon, ask yourself if the material that follows the colon serves one of these four functions:

- it contains a list (with exceptions noted as follows)
- it elaborates what has gone before
- it illustrates a rule or principle
- it starts a quotation

### The colon and the list.

Use a colon when introducing a series, whether commas, semicolons, numbers, or bullets connect the items.

Example:

They carried the most varied burdens: a bed in sections came out of Mallards passing on its way sections of another bed from the Cottage; bookcases were interchanged and wardrobes; an ant festooned with gay water-color sketches made his brilliant progress towards Mallards, meeting another who carried prints of Mozart at the age of four improvising on the spinet and of Beethoven playing his own compositions to an apparently remorseful audience.

Note: In the example above, notice how the items in the list are separated not by commas but by semicolons. Why is that? Because several of the items have their own internal punctuation (other commas) and so semicolons—not commas—are used to show the reader the conclusion of each item's description.

**Important exceptions:** Do not use a colon after verbs or prepositional phrases such as *includes; including; including, but not limited to; consists of; such as;* and *for example*. Because phrases like these already indicate to the reader that a list of items or examples will follow, there is no need to introduce the list with a colon, which would be redundant. However, if the introductory clause ends with an expression like *as follows* or *the following*, you must follow with a colon.

This is incorrect: We consider it our privilege to represent clients from many different industries, including: [a list follows]

This is incorrect: This website provides current information including: the opinions, court docket, court calendars, administrative orders, oral arguments and other useful facts regarding Florida's Second District Court of Appeal.

(And that sentence doesn't use the serial comma either...not good writing at all.)

Most of the time, you'll need to put a comma *in front of* "including" and "such as" and the parenthetical information that follows, especially if that information is a list of three or more items.

Example: As a consulting principal, Tony has advised a number of organizations, including Symantec, CSC, Gartner, and MasterCard.

Example: Bruce has more than 25 years' experience in enterprise b-to-b sales and marketing, including ten years running the predictive analytics business that he founded.

## Bullet points and lists.

Bullet points are a rather new convention, made popular by word processors. Their use is restricted to business writing, as opposed to fiction, and they can and do make lists look clean and straightforward. There are several things to be careful about when using bullet points:

- be sure to follow the "Important exceptions" above.
- keep each point's structure the same (i.e., don't switch verb tense).
- have at least three related items in the list.
- don't use commas or semicolons to connect the points.
- use phrases or full sentences, but not a mix; in other words, either end all of your points with a period (if each point, coupled with the introduction, constitutes a full sentence) or use phrases instead, but don't mix it up.

Here's an example of a properly presented bullet point list.

There were three things I learned from my grandmother that are still valuable today:

- When meeting someone for the first time, remain neutral. Don't trust the person, don't *distrust* the person—remain neutral until the person's character reveals itself.
- Send a hand-written thank-you note within a week after the receipt of a gift or favor.

- Never call the boy.

Here's a good example of what a bullet point list should *not* look like. The introductory sentences are quoted to give context.

Charles Schwab and Charles Schwab Institutional are registered trademarks of Charles Schwab & Company, Inc. Our company is independent and not employed by or an agent of Charles Schwab & Company, Inc.

- 30 years of professional money management
- Exceed the return of the S&P 500, including dividends, over each five year period.
- Monthly, semiannual, and annual communications
- Payment of management fee is contingent on Client's complete satisfaction
- Provide a higher degree of safety than stocks in general.

Each of these five items is supposed to demonstrate a benefit that this particular company's clients receive, but there is no continuity of style or focus that makes this list anything more than an awkward, rather unrelated group of statements. Plus, there are a number of mistakes that further confuse: two of the five points conclude with a period, even though the points are not full sentences; "five year period" should be hyphenated to read "five-year period"; *clients* is capitalized and it shouldn't be; and there seems to be a missing word in that same point because it looks as though that concept should read "each client's."

Would you trust these people with your financial future?

Ah, the Florida Bar. Look at this!

Jurors should not.....

- Do any outside research or google the defendant or witnesses in a trial;
- Be influenced by outside pressures or public opinion about the case;

• Decide cases based on prejudice, bias, or sympathy;

• Decide cases based on their feelings about the lawyers.

Do not bother with semicolons between bullet points. And why is "google" not capitalized? Last time I looked, Google is a proper noun *and* verb.

**The colon and elaboration.**

Use a colon to join two parts of a sentence when you wish to use the second part to emphasize, illustrate, explain, or summarize the first.

Often, the test of whether or not to use a colon depends on whether (or not) you can substitute the word *namely*, or, sometimes, the phrase *that is* or *that is to say* for the colon. Even though this is not a completely hard-and-fast rule, try those substitutions for the colon in the following examples and see how often they do work.

The purpose of driving the Lamborghini was simple: to go fast.

The purpose of driving the Lamborghini was simple [namely] to go fast.

I read this style guide for one purpose: to master punctuation rules.

I read this style guide for one purpose [namely] to master punctuation rules.

Suddenly the solution of her present difficulty flashed upon her: Riseholme.

Suddenly the solution of her present difficulty flashed upon her [namely] Riseholme.

"There's no organization at present, you see: great fun, but no organization."

"There's no organization at present, you see [that is to say] great fun, but no organization."

There's nothing going on: there's none of the old fizz and bubble and Excelsior there used to be.

There's nothing going on [that is to say] there's none of the old fizz and bubble and Excelsior there used to be.

Other examples:

About the question of connubialities, he meant to be quite definite: it must be a *sine qua non* of matrimony, the first clause in the marriage treaty, that they should be considered absolutely illicit, and he need not waste thought over that. [emphasis with elaboration]

Let's concentrate: that means thinking of nothing at all. [explanation]

"If you cannot promise to be always by me for my guidance and support, I can only give one answer: an unqualified negative." [emphasis]

Though it was close to the road, it was not overlooked, for a thick hedge of hornbeam made a fine screen: besides, the road did not lead anywhere in particular. [summary]

The "namely" rule works wonderfully well at the introduction of a list: the introduction of a list is the most obvious example of when you just have to use a colon.

**The colon and a rule or principle.**

Use a colon when quoting a rule or principle.

Example:

All too often I look at a politician and think of the Peter Principle: People are promoted to the level of their incompetence.

Note: Capitalize the word following the colon when quoting a rule or principle.

**The colon and a quotation.**

A colon also introduces a quotation, whether short or long. This is not the same as introducing dialog, which is most often introduced by a comma.

## This is incorrect:

In the words of Benjamin Franklin, "by failing to prepare, you are preparing to fail."

This is correct:

In the words of Benjamin Franklin: "By failing to prepare, you are preparing to fail."

**Other uses of a colon.**

Use a colon to separate the chapter and verse in a biblical reference.

Example: My favorite Bible passage is Romans 8:31-39.

Use a colon to separate the hour and minute(s) in a time notation: 8:17 p.m.; 2:11 a.m.

Acts and scenes of plays can be separated by a colon.

Example: *Hamlet*, III:v

**Spaces and capitalization with a colon.**

There are no spaces when a colon is sandwiched between two numbers. Authors used to place two spaces after a colon in a sentence, but it seems we've moved away from that practice and now there's only one space (though there are still style guides that dictate two spaces after periods and colons; you might want to check with your teacher or professor to find out what the preferred style is).

Use a colon to separate the title of a book from its subtitle: *The Complete Biography Workbook with Two Templates: The fun and easy way to write and publish your autobiography.*

If the material following the colon constitutes a full sentence, some style manuals suggest capitalizing the first word of the sentence. If the material following the colon is a dependent clause or phrase, do not capitalize the first word. If the material that follows the colon is rule or principle, or if the word that follows is a proper noun, the text should begin with a capital letter.

**Colon don'ts.**

Do not use a colon between a preposition, such as *of, by,* or *in,* and its object.

Do not put a colon between a verb and its object.

Don't use more than one colon in a sentence.

**Colons and dashes.**

Sometimes, but not always, an author will choose to use a dash as opposed to a colon to provide emotional or dramatic emphasis to the material that follows the introduction.

Example: "Lemme introduce myself and friend—Major Flint, that's me, and my friend Captain Puffin."

**Colons versus semicolons.**

A colon is a mark of *introduction*; a semicolon is a mark of *linking.* A semicolon replaces a comma + a conjunction in linking two complete sentences.

## Commas.

The misplaced comma is far and away the most common punctuation error we see. Commas, it seems, are placed in a sentence like the tail in a game of Pin the Tail on the Donkey, when the player strikes out blindly, hoping for the best.

Commas *separate.*

There are three basic uses of a comma:

- Commas separate sections of a sentence.
- Commas separate ancillary information from the body of the sentence.
- Commas separate items in a list.

**Commas separate sections of a sentence.**

Commas are used in two ways to separate sections of a sentence: they precede coordinating conjunctions, and they follow introductory phrases and adverb clauses.

Commas are used to separate independent clauses joined by *but, and, or, nor, for,* and, from time to time, *yet* and *so.* Those words (which can form the acronym FANBOYS if you need a memory aid) are called coordinating conjunctions. An independent clause—also known as a main clause—is a group of words that has a subject and a verb and can stand alone as a complete sentence.

The sentence structure will look like this:

main clause + COMMA + coordinating conjunction + main clause

Example: He looked quite bronzed, and she gave him the warmest welcome.

Sometimes, however, if the sentence is very short and the clauses are closely connected, the comma can be omitted.

Example: It is the rainy season and my garden looks lovely.

**When a sentence begins with *but, and, so, or, nor, for,* and *yet,* sometimes—but not always—it is appropriate to follow that word with a comma.**

Examples:

So, instead of lying down and taking aspirin and dozing, she set out after lunch to walk it off.

But however enjoyable it all might be, she appeared to herself at least to be suffering tortures of suspense, through which by degrees an idea, painful and revolting in the extreme, yet strangely exhilarating, began to insinuate itself into her mind.

**Commas do not separate *but* when it is followed by *which* or *for*.**

Example: The wall would have fallen but for the trusses.

Commas are not used when the interjected phrase is "not...but," "not...just," or "not only...but."

Examples:

As far as my dream car goes, I not only want the top-of-the-line Porsche 911 Turbo S Cabriolet but I want it in a special color called Amethyst Metallic.

I've always been the naturally nervous type, so I bought not one wedding dress but three.

If, however, such a phrase seems to require special emphasis or clarification (usually a matter of editorial discretion), you may use commas to set off the "not" phrase. Alternatively, a dash may be used in place of the first comma.

Example: I was sorry to hear he'd gone to the pokey to serve a five-to-seven stretch—not only because he was a pretty good guy, but also because he owed me a fair amount of money.

**Commas can be used to introduce.**

If a sentence begins with an introductory word, phrase, or adverb clause, a comma should follow that word or phrase.

A comma generally, though not always, follows introductory words and phrases and adverb clauses. Oftentimes, the "introductory" word or phrase begins with a subordinate conjunction, such as *although, as, as far as, as if, as soon as, as though, because, before, even if, even though, how, if, in order (that), in that, inasmuch as, insofar as, lest, next, now once, provided that, that, since, so, so that, than, that, 'til, such as that, supposing, supposing that, though, unless, until, what, when, whenever, where, whereas, whether, while, which, who, why.*

Introductory clauses are dependent clauses that provide background information or "set the stage" for the main part of the sentence: the independent clause. An introductory word or phrase defines or limits the scope of the sentence.

Here is the general construction:

Introductory word/phrase + COMMA + subject + predicate

Adverb clause + COMMA + main clause

Examples:

"By the way, Georgie, Irene takes so much interest in your painting."

However, there it was.

To begin with, it was only this morning that the baseness of Elizabeth in the matter concerning the Art Committee had come to light.

If so, that was a great mistake; Tilling did not want to witness a demonstration of forgiveness or white feathers, but a combat without quarter.

If they want to be successful, writers must write every day.

Because she loves Lamborghinis, Liz has a poster of a 1998 Lamborghini Diablo Roadster VT taped to her office wall.

In general, if the subordinate conjunction and its clause *follow* the main clause, do not use a comma.

Reversing the order of the clauses in the sentences above, you have:

Writers must write every day if they want to be successful.

Liz has a poster of a 1998 Lamborghini Diablo Roadster VT taped to her office wall because she loves Lamborghinis.

If, however, the content of the clause following the subordinate conjunction is parenthetical in nature—that is, not necessary—use a comma.

Examples:

There are certain processes of mental solidification which take place with extraordinary rapidity, because the system is already soaked and supersaturated with the issues involved.

Degrading, too, as were the records of Lucia's movements in the columns of Hermione, Riseholme had been thrilled (though disgusted) by them, because they were about Lucia, and though she was coming down for a complete rest (whatever that might mean)...

Mrs. Brocklebank had said that in two or three days she hoped to be able to see her friends again, and that fitted beautifully, because in two or three days now the Contessa's visit would have come to an end, and...

An exception to this no-comma-if-subordinate-conjunction-clause-follows-main-clause rule happens when the subordinate clause expresses a contrast, such as clauses beginning with *whereas* and most clauses beginning with *although.*

Example: Her work there was done, whereas here, as this week of influenza testified, there was a very great deal to do.

Use commas following introductory words like *however, still, furthermore*, and *meanwhile* to create continuity from one sentence to the next.

When a sentence starts off with an adverb such as *however, therefore*, and *indeed*, a comma traditionally follows. However, when the adverb is essential to the meaning of the clause, or if no pause is intended or desired, commas are not needed.

Example: However you need to do it, get it done.

**Commas to introduce a list.**

When a word or phrase like *includes, including,* and *such as* introduces a list, most of the time a comma will precede its use.

Examples:

Clients may ask for this change in rate for several reasons, including an increase in the rate for job complexity, a decrease in the rate for a bulk order, a substantial change in the job specifications.

I have many of the skills you are looking for, such as creativity, passion, and attention to detail.

**Commas within a list.**

Commas are used to separate items in a list, if the items themselves contain no internal punctuation. (When the items do contain internal punctuation, use a semicolon to separate items. Read the "Semicolons and commas in lists" section that follows for more discussion.) Use commas carefully within a list, because without a comma to separate items there is an implied relationship between any items not separated by a comma.

Example: My diet at this time consisted largely of soy burgers, a very little fruit, rice and beans.

In this example, the implication is that the "rice and beans" were mixed.

If that is not the case, then this sentence would be better expressed—more clear to your readers—if it was written like this:

My diet at this time consisted largely of soy burgers, a very little fruit, rice, and beans.

If your diet did consist of a mixture of rice and beans, then a better way to write this sentence would be:

My diet at the time consisted largely of soy burgers, a very little fruit, and rice and beans.

**In praise of the serial comma.**

Creating confusion is not what an author wants to do. A comma after the second-to-the-last item in a list—which is called a "serial" or "Oxford" comma—is entirely appropriate and helps with clarity, especially if the last item joined by "and" falls into another line.

Example:

The school also allows students to focus on career tracks in Finance, International Business, Management, Marketing and Sports Management.

Question: Does the school offer a degree in "Marketing and Sport Management," or does the school offer separate degrees in "Marketing" and "Sports Management"?

Gee, that's a good question! Do you see how this can be confusing to your readers? (As it happens, the school offers two separate degrees in Marketing *or* Sports Management, but you sure couldn't be 100% certain without that last comma.)

Here's another example, from the internet via accessHollywood:

"Big, bold, full and dark brows that accentuate the shape of your face," are the big trend in brows right now, according to celebrity eyebrow expert Tonya Crooks, who has worked her magic on Megan Fox, Gwyneth Paltrow, Fergie and Eva Mendes.

Ignoring, for the moment, those first four adjectives, let's look at the four women listed at the end of this sentence.

Not being totally in the know about the latest celebrities, when I read this I thought, *Fergie? The Duchess of York? No, it couldn't be. Eva Mendes must have a sister:* Fergie *Mendes!*

I later found out that "Fergie" is a celebrity, so this does not refer to a) the Duchess of York, or b) a sister (or mother, or aunt, or niece, or pet gerbil) of Eva Mendes, but don't you see how neglecting that serial comma can cause confusion?

The serial comma rule applies to lists with both *and* and *or*.

The serial comma issue is huge. Everyone has an opinion. Many authorities (mostly people with a newspaper background) are against it, but in the same breath will go on to say that it should be used when it helps readers. So, sometimes it should be used, but sometimes not. That is not an acceptable stance, leading as it does to not-consistency or non-continuity, or however you want to phrase it. If it helps once, it helps every time.

My take on this matter is simple: A comma or a semicolon should separate every item in a list. Period.

**One more thing about lists.** Don't lard up your lists. When you say "including this, this, and that," don't follow the list with "among others," "to name a few," or some similar phrase. "Including" already means that you're not providing a complete list, so you don't have to add "among others." We know that already because you used "including."

## Using etc. and et. al. in a list.

"Etc." is used to indicate that only some of the items in a list have been used. When "etc." is used in the middle of a sentence, it is *always* followed by a comma.

Example: Ferraris, Maseratis, Lamborghinis, Aston Martins, etc., are types of exotic cars.

However, if "etc." appears at the end of a sentence, then the period (which is part of "etc.") serves as the final punctuation mark.

Example: My autobiography workbook has been featured in the *Miami Herald*, the *Palm Beach Post*, the *Ocala Banner-News*, the *Ft. Myers News-Press*, the *Athens* [Georgia] *Banner-Herald, Florida Today,* etc.

A location not part of the title can be included using brackets or parentheses.

Or, since "etc." is not a particularly graceful addition to any sentence, that sentence could be written like this:

My autobiography workbook has been featured in many magazines and newspapers, including the *Miami Herald,* the *Palm Beach Post,* the *Ocala Banner-News,* the *Athens* [Georgia] *Banner-Herald* and *Florida Today.*

The same rule holds true for et al.

The abbreviation "et al.," which means "and others," can follow a list of people who are too numerous to mention, whether used in regular text, or (as is more common) in bibliographical references, or in the styling of multiple parties to a lawsuit, and should be treated like "etc." If et al. follows a single item, however (e.g., "Coursen et al."), it requires no preceding or following comma.

## Semicolons and commas in lists.

Use a semicolon to join elements in a list when at least one item in the list already includes a comma or some other form of internal punctuation.

Example:

She dropped her sketch; she reached out a trembling hand for her opera glasses, the focus of which was already adjusted to a nicety; and by their aid she saw that this athletic wasp who was skipping with such exuberant activity was none other than the invalid.

However, interior punctuation is not always necessary when creating a series of items, actions, or thoughts with sufficient connection and sufficient contrast; use a semicolon when the list reveals a striking contrast to what went before.

Example: Elizabeth Mapp was still in action and capable of delivering broadsides; innumerable crises might arise; volcanoes smoked;

thunderclouds threatened; there were hostile and malignant forces to be thwarted.

**Commas enclose parenthetical portions of a sentence.**

A parenthetical portion gives an explanation or comment, and commas provide a slight break. If a stronger break is needed or if there are commas within the parenthetical element, then dashes or parentheses should be used.

Read these three sentences out loud and listen to the subtle differences in the way you pause while reading them:

Luck, as usual, befriended ability.

Luck—as usual—befriended ability.

Luck (as usual) befriended ability.

One easy way to determine the "parenthetical" portion of a sentence is that when the content between the commas is removed, the sentence reads fine. Consider the sentences that follow.

Example: "Luck, as usual, befriended ability..."

The parenthetical portion, "as usual," can be removed and the sentence still makes sense: "Luck befriended ability."

Example: Diva, who had seen her from the window, flew to open it.

This could also have been written "Diva flew to open it."

**Commas aren't used in restrictive clauses or phrases.**

A restrictive clause provides information that is essential to the meaning of the sentence and is usually introduced by *that* (or *who, whom*, and *whose*). A restrictive clause is never set off by commas.

A phrase that is restrictive—that is, essential to the meaning (and often the identity) of the noun it belongs to—should not be set off by commas.

Examples:

The silver Lamborghini was the one that I needed to drive to the party because my black Lamborghini was in the shop.

I am the person who was driving the Lamborghini.

Here's a situation where someone has more than one brother and needs to specify which one likes to fly fish.

My brother Steven loves to go fly fishing.

If, in the sentence above, the writer has only one brother, you'd write the following: My brother, Steven, loves to go fly fishing.

This sentence is incorrect:

Prior to joining SiriusDecisions, Brad was Vice President of Marketing for the global technology solutions firm, ROLTA, where he led marketing for the Americas, Europe, and MENA regions.

The name is the firm—ROLTA—is essential to the meaning of this sentence, and so there should be no comma between "firm" and "ROLTA." However, the comma after ROLTA, which precedes parenthetical information, is correct.

The sentence should read:

Prior to joining SiriusDecisions, Brad was Vice President of Marketing for the global technology solutions firm ROLTA, where he led marketing for the Americas, Europe, and MENA regions.

**Commas are used in nonrestrictive clauses.**

Nonrestrictive clauses are usually introduced by *which* (and *who, whom,* and *whose* and, sometimes, *when* and *where*), and contain information that is unnecessary (but interesting). Nonrestrictive clauses are set off from the rest of the sentence by commas (or, if at the end of a sentence, preceded by a comma).

Example: I didn't eat the oysters, which I adore, because I wasn't sure if they were fresh.

Example: Prior to joining our company, Bruce spent two years as the SVP of client success at Bulldog Solutions, where he was directly responsible for the satisfaction, growth, revenues, and profit of the company's installed base.

Example: Liz Coursen, of Sarasota, Florida, is an author, speaker, and an entrepreneur.

**Important note.** Watch that comma after "Florida": Commas are always placed after the state (or country, like ...Tours, France,...), as well as after the city or town.

If you are confident that people will understand where you're talking about without specifying the state, you could write:

Liz Coursen, of Sarasota, is an author, speaker, and an entrepreneur.

Note: I don't mean to sound critical of the good folks at the Associated Press, but I do want to say that I strongly disagree with them about two points. One point is the serial comma issue. The other point is that there are many American cities that the *AP Stylebook* says do not need to be accompanied by their respective states, cities like Dallas, Boston, Miami, Los Angeles, and so on. One of those cities is Washington. *AP* says that it is all right to simply say Washington, and leave off the D.C. I say that the city of Washington *must be* accompanied by D.C., to distinguish it from the state of Washington. If this is all about clarity, then the city of Washington must be written Washington, D.C.

Take a look at this sentence:

Rich spent 14 years at Gardner Group, most recently as executive vice president where his responsibilities included worldwide sales, marketing and events.

Since I do like a serial comma, let's add one after "marketing." You could certainly put a period after "executive vice president," because the author chooses to add the information about Rich's responsibilities, which is clearly parenthetical. I would suggest adding a comma after "executive vice president," so the sentence would read:

Rich spent 14 years at Gardner Group, most recently as executive vice president, where his responsibilities included worldwide sales, marketing, and events.

**A comma with "too"—your decision.**

The word "too" is an adverb that indicates "also" or "in addition." "Too" often shows up in the middle or at the end of a sentence. Most of the time you probably won't use a comma with "too" because your sentences will be chugging right along without the need for a pause. So you could say, "I too like reading mysteries" or "I like reading mysteries too." If, on the other hand, you want to emphasize an abrupt change of thought, you do use a comma, which, among other things, is used to indicate a pause: "I, too, like reading mysteries," or "I like reading mysteries, too." In these sentences, you are adding a pause to create emphasis.

There is no right or wrong here. The decision to use a comma or not before or after "too" is really up to you and is determined by the context of the paragraph where the "too" sentence is. If you want to emphasize your thought, you can add the comma to slow the sentence down. If no emphasis is necessary, then don't use a comma.

**Commas and quotation marks.**

In American English, commas (and periods!) always go *inside* quotation marks, whether double or single quotation marks. There. Are. No. Exceptions. This sentence, for example, is incorrect:

Within five business days of the "Payment Date", you can vicw the payment within your CreateSpace Member Account.

**Use a comma after a mild interjection.**

Example: Oh, I'll be okay.

**Commas, commas, everywhere....**

Here are a few rules to avoid using unnecessary commas (or, using them when they are necessary).

A second subject in a sentence triggers a comma after the first complete sentence and before the conjunction.

Incorrect: My dog is a rescue and I know I made the right decision to adopt her.

Correct: My dog is a rescue, and I know I made the right decision to adopt her.

Also correct:

My dog is a rescue; I know I made the right decision to adopt her.

My dog is a rescue. I know I made the right decision to adopt her.

Without a change of subject, a comma is generally unnecessary.

Incorrect: My dog is a rescue, and never misses a meal.

Do not use a comma to separate the subject from its verb, the verb from its object, or an adjective from its noun.

## The Coordinate Adjective Rule.

Here's a two-step test to decide whether or not you need a comma between two adjectives.

First, can you place *and* between the adjectives and have the phrase still make sense? (Note: I did not say *sound good;* I said *make sense.*)

Second, can you switch the order of the adjectives and still have a phrase that makes sense?

If so, you need a comma. If not, no comma.

Consider these phrases: a large dining room, a fancy riding school, a fast-moving cold front

A large *and* dining room makes no sense. No comma.

A fancy *and* riding school makes no sense. No comma.

A cold *and* fast-moving front makes no sense. No comma.

In sentences you'd write:

We have a large dining room.

She attended a fancy riding school for many years.

His prediction of a fast-moving cold front was dead wrong.

Consider these phrases: easily replicated unique businesses, a long-haired black cat, a 10-carat pear-shaped diamond

Franchising is a pathway to rapid growth for unique *and* easily replicated businesses makes sense. Comma.

A black *and* long-haired cat makes sense. Comma.

Pear-shaped *and* 10-carat diamond makes sense. Comma.

Let's go back to that long bit of information about celebrities and their eyebrows:

"Big, bold, full and dark brows that accentuate the shape of your face," are the big trend in brows right now, according to celebrity eyebrow expert

Tonya Crooks, who has worked her magic on Megan Fox, Gwyneth Paltrow, Fergie and Eva Mendes.

For clarity, I say this sentence needs a serial comma to separate the four names at the end. Okay. However, let's look at that first group of four adjectives: "big, bold, full and dark."

All these adjectives could be mixed up and put in any order and still make sense, so a comma should separate each one. Or, another way to write this would be to make the four items into two pairs, like this: "Big and bold, full and dark."

It would be up to the author to decide in what order to display the adjectives. Or, going back to the "'and' equivalency" concept, pick the two adjectives that are the most different and only use adjectives that are truly necessary. Because of the nice alliteration, I'd go with "big and bold," and leave it at that. Enough about eyebrows.

Do not use commas after a conjunction. (Well, go easy on them, anyway.)

In general, don't use a comma in front of *because*. Remember the rule: Dependent clause + comma + independent clause. Much of the time, *because* introduces a dependent clause.

Correct: Because of the weather, we stayed overnight.

Incorrect: We stayed overnight, because of the weather.

Correct: We stayed overnight because of the weather.

Do not use a comma to set off a restrictive clause or phrase. If the information is essential to the meaning of the sentence, you don't need a comma (or commas). Another way to say this is: Do not use commas to set off words (or short phrases) that are not parenthetical.

Examples:

My dog, Grace, is brown. (Because I have only one dog, I'd use commas.)

My dog Grace is brown. (Here I am specifying which of my dogs is brown because I have more than one dog.)

My husband, Steve, got lost. (There's no doubt about the identity of my husband, and removing "Steve" still gives us a complete sentence: My husband got lost.)

Last year, my daughter Eve got married, and my daughter Laura got divorced. (No commas around the names because you have to specify which daughter was married and which was divorced.)

Note: there is a growing trend to do away with commas around a name if, a) it comes after the title, and b) the title and the name identify the same person. It will be a trend worth watching because it makes sense.

Examples:

My husband Steve got lost. (Why clutter up a sentence with punctuation that does not aid in understanding?)

My husband Steve and my daughter Eve got lost. (Here the author has one husband and one daughter; there is no ambiguity.)

This doesn't work if the name comes before the title:

Steve, my husband, and Eve, my daughter, got lost.

(In the sentence above, you really need those commas because you'd never write "Steve my husband and Eve my daughter got lost." You could, however, write "My husband and my daughter got lost.")

**Big problem!**

Watch your verb use in a sentence like this:

Your signature on the Agreement, and your first payment, give us the authority to begin the work.

With the commas, the subject is singular: "Your signature." Which means, of course, that the verb is singular, and should be "gives."

However, there's a deeper issue here with the sentence structure, since "Your signature" is the subject and is separated from its verb: to give. Bad! But, since both things (the first payment *and* the signature) are necessary before the authorization can occur, then "your first payment" should be part of the subject.

The sentence should read:

Your signature on the Agreement and your first payment give us the authority to begin the work.

Or, better:

Nothing. (What's the purpose of that sentence anyway?)

**Commas with dates.**

Do not use a comma with dates when the order is day, month, and year.

Example: I was born on 15 January 1959.

Do not use a comma between a month and year or between a season and a year.

**Commas vs. Semicolons in Compound Sentences**

A group of words that contains a subject and a verb and expresses a complete thought is called an *independent* (or *main*) clause. Sometimes, an independent clause stands alone as a sentence, and sometimes two independent clauses are linked together into what is called a *compound* sentence. Depending on the circumstances, one of two different punctuation marks can be used to link the independent clauses in a compound sentence: a comma or a semicolon.

**Using a comma in a compound sentence.**

Use a comma after the first independent clause when you link two independent clauses with one of the following coordinating conjunctions: *and, but, for, or, nor,* and, sometimes, *so* and *yet.*

Examples:

I am going to spend my day in the garden, and it will be fun.

I forgot my gloves, so I used his.

I enjoy gardening, and it does wonders for my mental health.

## Using a semicolon in a compound sentence.

The litmus test of semicolon use is simple: are both clauses independent; in other words, is each sentence on either side of the semicolon a *complete* sentence? If so, a semicolon is okay; if not, no.

Use a semicolon to join two sentences without using a conjunction. Using the previous sentences as examples, if you remove the conjunction, you'd use a semicolon instead of a comma:

I am going to spend my day in the garden; it will be fun.

I forgot my gloves; I used his.

I enjoy gardening; it does wonders for my mental health.

Use a semicolon when the second clause restates the first.

Example: She had never been better occupied and diverted; the place suited her, and it bristled with opportunities.

Use a semicolon to join two independent clauses when the second clause begins with a conjunctive adverb (*however, therefore, moreover, furthermore, thus, meanwhile, nonetheless, otherwise, consequently*, etc.) or a transition (e.g., *in fact, in other words, for example, that is, for instance, in addition, on the other hand, even so*).

Examples:

It rained heavily during the afternoon; however, we managed to have our picnic between showers.

Bill and Bob couldn't make it to the summit and back before dark; therefore, they decided to camp for the night before attempting to summit the next morning.

I am going home; moreover, I intend to stay there.

Use a semicolon when you link two independent clauses with no connecting words.

Examples:

I am going home; I intend to stay there.

It rained heavily during the afternoon; we managed to have our picnic anyway.

They couldn't make it to the summit and back before dark; they decided to camp for the night.

## The Dreaded Comma Splice.

When two independent clauses are separated by a comma with no coordinating conjunction, the result is called a "comma splice."

Incorrect:

He poured the wine, she drank it.

Corrections:

He poured the wine, and she drank it.

He poured the wine; she drank it.

## Commas, dashes, and parentheses.

Typically, commas provide a slight break, and the momentum of the action continues. Dashes indicate a bigger break, but the information inside the dashes relates directly to the action or conversation, and so the momentum continues. Parentheses are used when the information inside the parenthesis is something the author (or one of his or her characters) wants you to know or to point out to you about the situation at hand, so there's a remove to the information inside parentheses that separates the parenthetical information from the action. If you think about it, parentheses are impossible in conversation—written or spoken.

Read these three sentences out loud and imagine them in a text. How are they different?

Luck, as usual, befriended ability. (neutral "voice")

Luck—as usual—befriended ability. (voice of character)

Luck (as usual) befriended ability. (thought of author or character)

Here are some uses of these punctuation marks. Their use almost seems to be the kind of thing you hear, in addition to knowing the rules.

Examples:

He had no hesitation whatever in accepting Lucia's proposal to stand the charges of this expedition, for, as she had most truly said, it was undertaken in her interests, and naturally she paid (besides, she was quite rich) for its equipment.

But Georgie's absence (cheap at the cost) and her own invisibility by reason of influenza made a seemingly unassailable position and it was with a keen sense of exhilaration in the coming contest that she surveyed the arena.

After all, since everybody seemed so sorry that (as they imagined) he was soon to leave Tilling, they ought to be very much pleased to find that he was doing nothing of the kind.

It would serve Lucia right, it is true, but it was unworthy of him.

Only a foolish ingenuous child (and Elizabeth was anything but that) could have considered these as isolated phenomena.

His own stationery evidently, of which he had left a supply, without charge, for the use of his tenant.

(A case could be made for parentheses with the “without charge” clause, but not dashes.)

Some hitch might arise, the price Colonel Cresswell proposed might not come up to his expectations, though—God knew—he would not dream of haggling over any reasonable offer.

“Too lovely,” he said. “Colonel Cresswell has bought my house at Riseholme—such a good price—and now at last I shall be able to settle in London.”

Amelia said “Scusi,” which everybody understood—even Lucia might have understood that—and was silent for a space as she tore it open and began reading it.

**Very important point!**

The parenthetical material, be it enclosed by commas, dashes, or parentheses, is not part of the subject, insofar as subject-verb-pronoun agreement. Consider this sentence:

Because nothing on these sites—which are filled with sales oriented messages—compel them to stay.

Remove the parenthetical information. The subject of this sentence is *nothing*. Nothing is *singular*; compel is *plural*. (Plus, “sales oriented messages” needs a hyphen between sales and oriented.) So, this sentence should properly read:

Because nothing on these sites—which are filled with sales- oriented messages—compels them to stay.

Here's another example:

He, along with Richard and their research team have developed many of the best practice marketing models used in the industry today.

This sentence is missing a comma, and the verb should be singular because the subject is "he." I'm not sure about the "their" because I don't know who "their" is. Plus, I'd use a hyphen between "best" and "practice." It should read:

He, along with Richard and their research team, has developed many of the best-practice marketing models used in the industry today.

## Dashes.

There are two types of dashes: *en* dashes (the width of an "n") and *em* dashes (the width of an "m").

Modern usage has almost entirely removed the wall between the two, and, for the most part, you will see only the *em* dash used nowadays (including in this style guide). I would suggest using *em* dashes throughout your work; just make sure you have not inadvertently used some of both.

Dashes are most often used to set off or emphasize the content enclosed within dashes or the content that follows a dash. Dashes represent a stronger break in thought or activity than do commas, but less of a break than parentheses.

### Spaces with dashes.

At the moment, authorities differ about whether or not a space should precede and follow a dash, but the trend is against spaces. The *AP Stylebook* says to add a space both before and after a dash; other style guides say no space. The key thing is to be consistent.

### Creating dashes.

Some word processing and email programs do not support dashes, which are not part of a typical keyboard. There are two ways to create a dash: you can use the symbols function on your keyboard, or, if you use Microsoft Word, you can follow the directions below.

If you need a dash, here's what to do in Microsoft Word: type the preceding word, but don't use the space bar; type two hyphens, one after another with no spaces; don't skip a space; type the next word; and, most of the time, after you hit the space bar *after* the second word, Word will create a dash.

Using the symbols function (those numbers to the far right of your keyboard) goes like this: Turn on the Number Lock, hold down ATL, and press 0 1 5 1. Voilà!

**A dash isn't a dash when it's a hyphen.**

Using a hyphen instead of a dash (and vice versa) is unacceptable:

We are writing for humans - not robots.

At Merrill Lynch, your financial advisor focuses on the things you care about most- family, goals and priorities - even as they change over the years.

Using two hyphens as a substitute for a dash is *very* unacceptable. Here are two examples of this unfortunate practice.

At The ABC Agency, Jackie's works create an incredible and unique online presence for her clients--from inception to production launch to post-launch assessment.

There are a few legal documents that are especially important to life at our company -- to us, our customers, our prospects, and just plain old users of our website.

Using three hyphens, alas, is worse:

Please contact us to arrange a viewing of artwork at your convenience---during gallery hours or by private appointment.

**Use a dash to set off an appositive phrase that already includes commas.**

Example: The cousins—Tina, Jeff, and Kim—arrived at the party together.

**An effective use of the dash is in conversation, to indicate a mental pause or (as in this case) an attempt to distract.**

Example: "I have contracted to send all my garden produce to Twistevant's—such a quaint name, is it not?—for these months, and for the same reason I should be unable to supply this fête which I have heard spoken of."

**Dashes can also note a conversational aside.**

Example: "So good of you to let us come, dear Susan," she said. "I have very great experience in psychical phenomena: adepts—do you remember the Guru at Riseholme, Georgie?—adepts always tell me that I should be a marvelous medium if I had time to devote myself to the occult."

**Repetition of the previous word—to create a sort of stuttering when used in dialog—adds emphasis.**

Examples:

"We all run after distinguished people like—like Alf and Marcelle."

"I wouldn't have her on our museum committee if—if she gave her pearls to it and said they belonged to Queen Elizabeth."

"Lucia, I've got something I must say, and I hope you won't mind. Has it ever occurred to you that—well—that we might marry?"

**A dash indicates an interruption or a quick break in conversation or train of thought.**

Example:

"So I've asked her lover instead—"

“No!” said Marcia. “Go on.”

**Dashes can also be used to signify continuing dates, times, and numbers.**

Examples:

The workshop will take place on Saturday, October 15, 10:15 a.m.—3:30 p.m. (Note the space between the time and the a.m./p.m. There are no spaces on either side of the dash.

The years 2000—2006 were exciting ones in the real estate market.

My favorite version of the Christmas story is found in the King James Bible: Luke 2:1—14.

However, you do not use a dash if you use “from” to start the phrase. In that case you have to write from such-and-such to thus-and-so.

Example: I plan to be there anywhere from 4 o’clock to 5:30 p.m.

(Note: There’s always a space between the time and a.m./p.m.)

Also, if you say “between” you can’t use a dash; you must use “and” between the two numbers.

Example: I hope to score between ninety and ninety-five on the test.

**The dash is also used to indicate a range between places or numbers.**

Examples:

My weight bounces between 145—160, which I hate.

The New York—Rome leg of our journey should be fun, especially since we’re flying Alitalia: Alitalia always serves great food.

By contrast, a hyphen is used between numbers that are unchanging and do not indicate a range: sports scores, Social Security numbers, and telephone numbers are examples of when you'd use a hyphen, and not a dash.

**Dashes can also be used to indicate missing letters or to avoid using someone's name.**

Examples: I'll be d—if I will.

My former minister, Rev. P—, is known for his long-winded sermons.

## Let's test your knowledge!

What's wrong with these sentences? (Answers follow.)

1. John, along with Richard was one of the five officers of the company.

2. Mr. Kline is currently a member of the boards of several privately-held companies.

3. Insignia Bank is community banking at it's finest.

4. But what about that small voice that plagues you as you drive home from a meeting or awaken to start a challenging day, that voice that condemns your very effort before you even get started?

5. Open houses are still the best opportunity to get face-to-face with potential buyers and sellers. The presenter will show you how to use technology to market and host your open houses as well as give you new tools to take your costumer experience to the next level.

6. "We've underutilized these features up until this point, and we're looking forward to using them to help protect our customer's valuable time selling them what they need when they need it with less effort on their part," concludes James.

7. The unique benefits of our program for your brand includes:

- Dramatic improvement in organic rank for keywords people use to search for you
- Reflect seasonal communications or product changes that demonstrate your brand is "current"

- Protection from negative or harmful search results that may impact the credibility of your brand
- Increased visibility amongst secondary and tertiary keyword search results
- Direct communication with customers and clients to improve relationship and responsiveness
- Out positioning your competition with thought-leadership content with established voice and immediacy

8. This eye-opening session will provide insights info how Steve has contracted and delivered 584 paid speaking engagements in the last five years.

9. The Head of Content is a leader with deep experience and passion for working with creative and product management teams to take the organizations key asset, its expert content and content/video production methods, to the next level.

10. Our clients' benefit from this relationship by receiving regular monthly statements from Charles Schwab Institutional, they can also access and view all accounts on-line using the Charles Schwab web site..

11. It's great being apart of such a caring team!

## Answers:

1. You need a comma after Richard because the phrase "along with Richard" is parenthetical.

2. Never hyphenate an *-ly* adverb, so no hyphen between *privately* and *held.*

3. The old it's versus its mistake strikes again!

4. Oops, shouldn't that read *every*, and not *very*?

5. Well, I'd want a comma before the phrase "as well as," and I know the writer means *customer*, not costumer: Open houses are still the best opportunity to get face-to-face with potential buyers and sellers. The presenter will show you how to use technology to market and host your open houses, as well as give you new tools to take your customer experience to the next level.

Note: "To the next level" is a cliché—avoid it.

6. The phrase "up until" is incorrect; "up to this point" or "until this point" would be correct. Plus, there's a big problem with "customer's," which is singular possessive, and needs to be plural possessive: customers'. Last, but not least, we risk confusion by using the pronoun "them" twice in the sentence to refer to two different things. The first use of "them" refers to the features, and the second use refers to customers.

7. Lots of little things condemn this bullet point list:

- "Unique benefits" include, not includes
- There shouldn't be a colon after "includes"
- *Negative* and *harmful* are nearly synonymous; one or the other but not both
- Don't use *amongst* in America; use *among*
- *Customers* and *clients* are nearly synonymous; one or the other but not both
- The phrase "out positioning" is not great, especially leading off the point; at a minimum, it needs a hyphen
- The phrase "thought-leadership" should be banned

8. *Info* is *into* misspelled; plus, the phrase *contracted and delivered* would not have been my first choice.

9. Here's a good example of being too concise, just a tad too edgy: you've got to have an article in front of *deep experience* or *passion* (or both). We're also missing an apostrophe in *organization*: the sentence should read *organization's.* Plus, say what you like, to take something *to the next level* is a phrase whose time has come...and gone. Corrected, it reads: The Head of Content is a leader with deep experience and a passion for working with creative and product management teams to take the organization's key asset, its expert content and content/video production methods, to the next level.

10. What an ugly bit of writing! This is a good example of a comma splice: there are actually *two* sentences here. *Clients* is plural, not possessive. *Online* doesn't need a hyphen. *Website* is one word. Corrected, the passage would read: Our clients benefit from this relationship by receiving regular

monthly statements from Charles Schwab Institutional; they can also access and view all accounts online using the Charles Schwab website. And TWO periods at the end of the sentence! Shoot me now.

11. Here's where a space is a deal-breaker: It's *a part*, not *apart*. *A part* mean to be a portion of the whole, while *apart* means separate. That would be a terrible mistake in a contract.

## Ellipses.

An ellipsis indicates a pause or a break in action, or a break or change in a train of thought, and is indicated by three sequential periods (which, in this context, are called "points").

**Using an ellipsis in the middle of a sentence.**

Ellipses can be used in the middle of a sentence: the first letter of the word that follows the ellipsis is not capitalized, unless it is a proper name. There are no spaces between the words that precede and follow the ellipsis.

Example: He had already taken the stopper out of the decanter when their eyes met...and then he put it back again.

**Using the ellipsis at the beginning of a phrase or sentence.**

Ellipses can be used at the beginning a sentence, to indicate that the thought or action has already begun.

If used at the beginning of a sentence, use three points.

**Using the ellipsis at the end of a phrase or sentence.**

Ellipses can be used at the end of a phrase or a sentence, when the thought or action "trails off."

If an ellipsis is used at the end of a phrase (not a full sentence), three points are used.

Example: With brazen effrontery Susan informed her daughter that Mr. Wyse thought a little leaf mold...

If, however, an ellipsis is used at the end of a complete sentence, use four points: the sentence's period plus the ellipsis.

Example: He ought to know, for Christmas (as was usual in December) was daily drawing nearer....

The same holds true when two sentences are joined together: the first sentence gets its period, and is followed by the ellipsis. When the ellipsis joins two sentences there are no spaces between the first and second sentences and the ellipsis. The first letter in the second sentence is capitalized.

Example: It occurred to her that the engagement might have been broken off....A little later, again with a quickened pulse, Miss Mapp saw the Royce lumber down from the church corner.

**The ellipsis with question marks and exclamation points.**

Question marks and exclamation points count as a mark of punctuation, and so are followed by a three-point ellipsis.

Example: Why then, thought Daisy with a sense of incredulous indignation, had Peppino come down a few Sundays ago, all by himself, and looking a perfect wreck?..."Very odd, I call it," muttered Daisy, turning over to her other side.

**The ellipsis with quotation marks.**

The following is another example of a three-point ellipsis joining two complete sentences, when the first sentence ends with quotation marks and the second sentence begins with quotation marks.

Example: She was visualizing herself in the modern world; she was going to be up to date; the music room in Brompton Square was not only to echo with the first movement of the "Moonlight."..."It's too thrilling," said

Georgie, as, warmed with this mental activity, he quite forgot to put on his fur tippet.

In dialog, to create a "trailing off" of conversation with a nuanced question embedded at the end of a sentence, a question mark can follow an ellipsis.

Example: "I knew her autobiography workbook would be a best seller," he said, "but who would have thought...?"

**Using the ellipsis when quoting poetry.**

If you are omitting a line or more of a poem, use a full line of ellipsis points:

> Whose woods these are I think I know,
> His house is in the village though;
> He will not see me stopping here
> To watch his woods fill up with snow.
> ...............................................
> The woods are lovely, dark, and deep,
> But I have promises to keep,
> And miles to go before I sleep,
> And miles to go before I sleep.
> —Robert Frost, "Stopping by Woods on a Snowy Evening"

(Interestingly, when you hold down the period symbol using Microsoft Word, the points automatically appear in groups of three.)

If a punctuation mark immediately follows the word where you start the ellipsis, include that mark. If a punctuation mark precedes the word where the ellipsis concludes, include that mark.

## Exclamation points.

Exclamation points can be used to indicate an emphatic or ironical comment, a high degree of surprise, incredulity, anger, or other strong emotion. For example, dialog when "screaming," "bellowing," or "shrieking" is involved demands an exclamation point.

Exclamation points can be used as often as is necessary, but sparingly, for all that, and should be reserved for the highest expression of emotion in that particular passage or scene.

**Exclamation points and dialog.**

The placement of an exclamation point depends on context.

Consider these two examples.

“I am going!” she shrieked.

“And that’s when he told me he ‘loved me’! Oh, can you believe it?”

If the spoken dialog includes an exclamation point, the exclamation point goes inside the quotation marks. If a character is quoting someone else, someone who did not use an exclamation point, but is emphasizing what it was that person said, then the exclamation point goes outside the quotation marks.

## Hyphens.

Hyphens are used for a number of purposes: to join words, to avoid confusion, and to marry a word with a prefix or suffix, like *self-*, *-is*, or *-related.*

Though authorities do not always agree in all cases, the uses of hyphens offered here are generally agreed upon. When in doubt about whether a word is hyphenated, is one word with no hyphen, or is two individual words, consult a newer edition of a dictionary.

**Compound nouns and adjectives versus compound verbs.**

Most of the time, you’ll see compound nouns and adjectives use hyphens (break-in, call-up, push-up, rip-off, send-off, shake-up, write-down, set-up), while compound verbs don’t (break in, call up, push up, rip off, send off, shake up, write down, set up).

Correct: I like the set-up. (compound noun)

Correct: Get set up within minutes. (compound verb)

If you think about it, the use of a hyphen will sometimes indicate a concept in flux, since a hyphen can be used to join two words, heretofore unrelated, to create a new word, a whole new taste sensation: mint-chocolate chip—not just mint, not just chocolate, but *mint-chocolate* chip. The time after noon becomes afternoon, a large section of bleachers, a grand stand, becomes a grandstand. The internet has spawned many new word combinations, including “electronic” and “mail”—two words that had nothing much to do with each other twenty years ago—which have been joined together to become “e-mail.” I feel it is time to take it one step further and drop the hyphen: email.

Oftentimes, two words brought together as a compound may be written separately, written as one word, or connected by hyphens. For example, three modern dictionaries all have the same listings for the following compounds:

hair stylist
hairsplitter
hair-raiser
life-like
water-front

Another modern dictionary, however, lists hairstylist, not hair stylist, and there are plenty of people who prefer lifelike to life-like and waterfront to water-front.

Sometimes the context of the story dictates the use. For example, an author could write about a man who was angry, a “mad man.” If the author meant to say that the man was mad, in the sense of insane, the author would write “madman.” A “mad man” is an angry man; a “madman” is an insane one.

Interestingly, even though most people have made the transition to “email,” not too terribly long ago the proper spelling was “e-mail,” and before that it was “E-mail.” The relatively new nouns “headshot” (a photo of someone’s head and shoulders for promotional purposes), “homepage,” “startup,” “keynote,” “website,” and “username” have made the single-word transition, according to many style guides, as have "proofread" and "copyedit" (which I don't particularly care for and won't use). The prefix *eco-* is still in a state of flux: ecosystem, but eco-friendly.

**Use a hyphen to join two or more words serving as a single adjective before a noun:**

There is a one-way stop sign at the end of Magnolia Street.

No one needs to eat chocolate-covered peanuts.

Liz hopes to become a well-known author.

The day-and-a-half class will cost $150.

Other examples: post-traumatic stress, queen-sized bed, high-quality tape, fifteen-minute pause, hip-hop exhibit, cutting-edge art, third-generation American.

This is incorrect:

Our recently released Worldwide Referrals Feature and this initiative are an important reminder that BNI is an innovative Member led organization that can have an incredible impact across the globe.

It should be "member-led organization." Since when is "member" a proper noun?

If there is a conjunction between the adjectives, hyphenate all words: prim-and-proper, spic-and-span, spit-and-polish, brighter-than-bright, suit-and-tie, prisoner-of-war, one-of-a-kind, rank-and-file, free-for-all, and so on.

There are more examples in the "Commonly Misspelled/Misused Words" section in Part 2.

Exception #1: do not hyphenate an adverb that ends in *-ly*, so that there is no hyphen between "badly" and "damaged": badly damaged. Other examples would be truly wicked, enormously influential, seriously strong.

These sentences are incorrect:

Join Members from across BNI USA at this nationally-facilitated event. (In addition to the incorrect hyphen, "members" is incorrectly capitalized.)

Ravnsborg nor his privately-hired public relations spokesperson responded to request for comment.

Perhaps most jaw-dropping: two newly-revealed near-misses with law-enforcement vehicles, as detailed in reports from the officers involved.

This next sentence—so pretentious—is wrong, wrong, wrong:

We help build digitally-driven businesses for some of the largest and most demanding companies in the world.

The hyphenated adverb mistake is really common—you see it all day long.

However! Not all words that end in *-ly* are adverbs. Here are three examples of hyphenated *adjectives*: family-friendly restaurant, friendly-looking professor, elegantly-electric attire (whatever that is).

Exception #2: do not use a hyphen between two modifying adjectives if they are part of a title, e.g., Gender Neutral Children's Clothing. Sometimes, but not always, the second word of a hyphenated word in a title is not capitalized: exceptions would be if the second word is a noun, a proper adjective, or if it is equal in importance to the first word.

**Important note!** Most of the time, when compound modifiers (whether one word or hyphenated, whether nouns or adjectives) come after the noun they modify, they **are not** hyphenated.

*Before* the noun:

If you don't mind getting kicked around now and then, and love data-driven, hard-core info, then you're going to become a fan of ConversionXL.

I do part-time work.

He's our hometown hero. (An example of a previously hyphenated word that has made the transition to a single word.)

*After* the noun:

You're going to become a fan of ConversionXL if you love info that's data driven and hard core.

I work part time.

He's a hero in his home town.

**Exceptions to the "Important note":**

Exception #1: In sentences when the verb is "to be," then the compound can be hyphenated following the noun.

Example: The bartender's countenance was ill-favored.

Exception #2: If you are using a familiar phrase as a noun or adjective, it is hyphenated regardless of its position in the sentence: stick-in-the-mud, hand-in-hand, one-on-one, mother-in-law, park-and-ride, pay-as-you-go, cover-up, good-for-nothing, hit-and-run, head-on, toe-to-toe, face-to-face, eyeball-to-eyeball.

## The Suspended Hyphen Rule.

When writing about two words that share the same suffix, regardless of whether the words use a hyphen, use a hyphen after the first part of the first word, skip a space, add the conjunction (typically *and*), and then follow with the second hyphenated word.

Examples: third- and fourth-place finishers, on- and off-site, upper- and lowercase letters, right- and left-brained thinking, pedestrian- and bike-oriented neighborhoods, high- and low-income cities, government- and state-run institutions, small- to medium-sized companies, brothers- and sisters-in-law, gain- and loss-framed messages

So this sentence, as written, is incorrect:

[He is an] Internet executive with over 19 years of experience, including general management of mid to large sized organizations, corporate development, product development, business operations, and strategy.

Some people are still capitalizing *Internet*. That's okay, for now. However, the sentence should be written like this:

[He is an] Internet executive with over 19 years of experience, including general management of mid- to large-sized organizations, corporate development, product development, business operations, and strategy.

If two words share the same suffix and one or both words are normally not hyphenated, you'll add a hyphen to the beginning of the first word and then spell out the second in its entirety: him- or herself, two- and tenfold.

Here's another incorrect sentence:

There are several ways you can integrate on and offline offers.

This should be written:

There are several ways you can integrate on- and offline offers.

This rule also applies when the words share the same beginning (which may not be a prefix in the traditional sense): Write the first, complete word, then the conjunction, and then begin the second word with a hyphen.

Examples: servicemen and -women, bridesmaids and -matrons, C-SPAN-1 and -2, on- and off-road vehicles, self-published and -promoted.

**Remember:** Hyphenated words are words that are in a state of flux. When in doubt, look it up!

**Hyphenated proper names.**

If you are referring to someone with a family background composed of two proper nouns, do not use a hyphen to connect the two words. *The AP Stylebook* equivocates on this important issue; however, both *The Chicago Manual of Style* and "The Princeton Editorial Style Guide" say no to hyphens for ancestral heritage compound nouns, and I agree. No hyphens as a stand-alone noun, no hyphens as a compound adjective. No hyphens, period.

This particular issue is the subject of much debate, so it is nice to take a stand.

However, use a hyphen to join a prefix or suffix to any capitalized noun: ex-Navy Seal, post-Civil War-era

**Hyphens and numbers.**

Hyphens are often necessary to separate numbers and words.

Use a dash to indicate a range between numbers, but use a hyphen to indicate a non-negotiable, unchangeable relationship between the two numbers, like in a score: Georgia Tech beat Duke 77-72 in a real thriller in 1998; it's a shame we can't do it every year!

Examples: 24-year-old, 264-page lawsuit, mid-1980s

Noun: the $20^{th}$ century; adjective: a $20^{th}$-century concept

(I personally think the *-th,* especially in the smaller font that Microsoft Word and other word processing programs automatically generate, coupled with a hyphen is awkward. This can be avoided by playing around with your word processor to create 20th century or by writing it all out: twentieth century.)

Hyphens, not dashes, separate Social Security numbers and telephone numbers.

Use a hyphen with compound numbers less than 100 and fractions, like forty-six, sixty-three, and four-fifths.

Even with all this discussion, the standard way to express numbers is to use words for numbers one through ten (one, two, etc.) and to write numerals for larger numbers (11, 12, 13, etc.).

What's wrong with this sentence, from Dictionary.com?

> You should also hyphenate numbers when they are part of larger numbers that are written out - but not other parts of large numbers, for example: 5,264 is written "five thousand two hundred sixty-four" and 523rd is written "five hundred twenty-third".

Actually, the concept about hyphenating numbers is fine, but there's a lot wrong with the sentence's punctuation. A lot. Let's see: that's a hyphen (with spaces!) and a dash should have been used between "out" and "but"; a semicolon, not a comma, is necessary before "for example"; and periods are *always* placed inside quotation marks in American English.

Here's another good example of an incorrect sentence, compliments of emory.edu:

> Located just east of Atlanta in Oxford, GA, Oxford College is a close knit community of sixty faculty, ninety staff, and nine-hundred students.

There is no hyphen between nine and hundred; GA (Georgia) should be spelled out; and "close-knit" is a compound adjective, requiring a hyphen. (Emory will say that its "style" is to use words for numbers, which is certainly okay, especially if the rest of the sentence is correct.)

I think that this sentence would be more correctly expressed:

> Located just east of Atlanta in Oxford, Georgia, Oxford College is a close-knit community of 60 faculty, 90 staff, and 900 students.

When two numbers are joined and one is part of a compound adjective, write one as a number and one as a word or words. Typically, the first number is written out, but if writing out the second number instead would significantly shorten the phrase, then the second number is written out.

Examples: eight $20 bills, two 4-piece bands, 45 two-page auction programs, 388 4- to 5-bedroom homes

What a difference a hyphen makes! Consider: twenty-first-row seats vs. twenty first-row seats. Look at the difference between these two situations:

I received a pair of tickets for twenty-first-row seats; I hope I'll be able to see the performers at that distance!

She bought a block of twenty first-row seats, which means we'll be close enough to see every little detail.

A hyphen is also used to describe ammunition: a .30-06 Springfield cartridge. (Here, the hyphen is pronounced "aught.")

**Hyphens and colors.**

The same general rules apply to writing about colors and their nouns.

Example: Liz buys size 9.5 black-and-white spectators on eBay.

This means Liz buys two-tone, spectator-style shoes that are black and white, i.e., both colors.

Example: Liz has a large collection of black and white shoes.

This means Liz has pairs of all-black shoes and pairs of all-white shoes in her collection. If there'd been hyphens in black-and-white, then Liz's collection would be made up of shoes with both colors in each pair.

The hyphen-before-modified-noun rule also applies to gradations of color.

Examples: a pair of brown-ish khaki pants, a green-khaki skirt, a light-gray dress, a chestnut-brown Bottega Veneta clutch

Remember: the underlying purpose of a hyphen is to avoid confusion, so watch when you say something like a "light lilac" jacket. A light lilac jacket is a purple jacket that is not necessarily very warm (it is "light"), while a light-lilac jacket is a jacket of unspecified warmth that is the color of pale lilac.

**Using hyphens when writing about weight and height**.

Example: a nine-pound, six-ounce baby

Example: a 135-pound adult

She was five feet, six inches tall. (Adjectives after the noun—no hyphens.)

Note: regardless of whether the height measurements are placed before or after the noun, the *AP Stylebook* does not use commas to separate feet from inches, but other authorities disagree.

He was a seven-foot, two-inch center: you can't coach seven feet! (Adjectives before the noun—hyphens.)

**Use a hyphen to avoid confusion or an awkward combination of letters, such as the doubling of the vowels "a" or "i," the repetition of a prefix, or the tripling of consonants:**

re-sign a petition (vs. resign from a job)

re-dress after a rain storm (vs. to seek redress after an injury)

re-elect, re-evaluate, re-establish, re-enact

I used both re-charge and re-place today after I forgot I had a new credit card and used the one on file. I had to ask the vendor if it could "re-charge"the new card or if I needed to "re-place" my order. "Recharge" and "replace" mean something totally different!

multi-ply paper towel (vs. multiply quickly)

semi-independent, semi-automatic (but semidelirious)

shell-like (but waiflike)

co-option (but cooperation)

biosphere (and, as strange as it looks: bioorganic)

Again, this is when consulting a recent edition of a dictionary can be invaluable. When in doubt, look it up.

## More uses of hyphens.

Use a hyphen with the prefixes *ex-* (meaning "former"); *self-; all-*; *anti-*; *half-; high-; quasi; hex-, mini-,* and *re-* (when *re-* precedes a word that starts with an "e"); with the suffixes *-style, -free, -based -type, -elect, -making,* and *-designate*; between a prefix and a capitalized word; and with figures or letters.

Use a hyphen before *-like* if the word being modified is two syllables or longer.

Use a hyphen before *-fold* if the number being modified is ten or greater: twofold versus ten-fold. However, if the numbers associated with *-fold* are single digits, use words for the numbers and only the first number gets a hyphen (three- and fivefold); if the numbers are not single digits, then use figures for the numbers and both get a hyphen (34- and 35.6-fold). (Who thinks up this stuff?)

On the rare occasion when the compound is composed of two words that end in *-ed*, drop the first *-ed*. So, it's the *freckle*-faced boy, not the freckled-faced boy.

Some examples of hyphenated compounds:

anti-Semitic (but Antichrist)

ex-convict, life-changing

air-conditioned (but air conditioning)

self-sufficient, ever-present

a mid-January thaw, the mid-1800s, a metro-Boston suburb

all-powerful, half-wit

after-dinner drink (but afterthought)

president-elect, vice-principal

anti-American (but transpacific, transatlantic)

C-suite, T-shirt, X-ray, U-boat, U-turn, A-frame, K-9, NC-17

pre-World War II, pre-WWII, twenty-odd years, mini-series

WXYZ-AM (all capitals)

## Prefixes and suffixes typically not hyphenated.

Keeping in mind the (many) exceptions listed above, here is a list of prefixes and suffixes that are typically not hyphenated: *aero, after, ante, anti, arch, auto, bi, bio, by, chemo, co, counter, cyber, di, electro, esque, exo, extra, hemo, hyper, hypo, geo, in, infra, inter, intra, ish, iso, ite, long, macro, maker, mega, meta, micro, mid* (note exceptions above), *mini, multi, neo, non, off, on, over, photo, physio, poly, post, pre, pro, proto, pseudo, re* (unless followed by a word that starts with an "e"), *semi, socio, sub, super, supra, time, trans, tri, ultra, un, under, uni, up, wide* (no hyphen as a suffix, but often hyphenated as a prefix), and *wise* (when in the sense of *with regard to* or *the direction of*). Remember: *eco-* is in flux.

Note: *The Chicago Manual of Style* is positively rude about the use of *-esque*. *Chicago* feels (strongly) that *-esque* should be used rarely, if at all, and when used there is no hyphen.

Here's an interesting rule having to do with the suffix *room*. If the word in front of *room* is two or more syllables, the compound noun is two words: living room, locker room, dining room. But, if the word is one syllable, one word is formed: bedroom, bathroom, and so on.

**Using hyphens to divide words at the end of a line.**

Use a hyphen to divide words at the end of a line if necessary, and make the break only between syllables:

pref-er-ence
sell-ing
in-di-vid-u-al-ist
Span-ish

For line breaks, divide already hyphenated words only at the hyphen.
Examples:
mass-
produced
self-
conscious

When a line breaks in words ending in *-ing*, if a single final consonant in the root word is doubled before the suffix, hyphenate between the consonants; otherwise, hyphenate at the suffix itself:
up-ping
run-ning
driv-ing

However: call-ing

Never put the first or last letter of a word at the end or beginning of a line, and don't put two-letter suffixes at the beginning of a new line.

Examples:

lovely (Do not separate to leave "ly" beginning a new line.)

eval-u-ate (Separate only on either side of the "u"; do not leave the initial "e-" at the end of a line.)

Of course, in this world of word processing and justified margins, a line break is almost entirely a thing of the past.

**Important note**. It should go without saying—which is why it's worth saying—that if you include a hyphen to break a line when writing the name of a website when there is no hyphen in the website's name, the hyphen will spin people off into the ozone....Do not allow a hyphen to be inserted in a website address when there is no hyphen there.

## I.E. vs. E.G.

The abbreviation i.e. refers to the Latin phrase *id est*, which means "that is," or "in other words." The abbreviation e.g. is short for *exempli gratia*, which means "for example."

Example: The main performance difference between the Porsche 911 Turbo and the 911 Turbo S (i.e., two miles per hour top speed) is indistinguishable to all but the most sophisticated driver.

Example: Italian cars (e.g., Alpha Romeos, Ferraris, Lamborghinis) are notoriously undependable, and British cars (e.g., Aston Martins, Jaguars, Bentleys, and Rolls-Royces) aren't much better.

This is not an acceptable substitute for e.g.:

The data you collect can also drive your strategic decision making. Ex: Determining resources vs. volume of hiring.

This should have been written:

The data you collect can also drive your strategic decision making (e.g., determining resources vs. volume of hiring).

This is also an incorrect use:

What is the primary purpose of producing the ebook, e.g.: create awareness/generate leads/brand building?

This sentence could have been written in either of these two ways:

What is the primary purpose of producing the ebook (e.g., create awareness, generate leads, brand building)?

What is the primary purpose (e.g., create awareness, generate leads, brand building) of producing the ebook ?

Both i.e. and e.g. are best used within parentheses. A comma *always* follows their use, as seen in the examples above, so this next sentence from eBay is incorrect: You made a mistake when entering your bid, e.g. $50 instead of $5.

And, despite the title of this section, they are never capitalized.

## Indenting.

Indenting is a stylistic convention designed to let your reader know when you've changed the focus of your writing.

Most writers, especially fiction writers, will indent the first line of each paragraph four or five spaces. (Be consistent: four *or* five.)

When writing dialog, every time the speaker changes you should indent to maintain clarity.

It is appropriate to indent at the beginning and end of a speech or long quote. See the section about Quotations for the general rules.

## It.

The pronoun *it* can come in very handy. Just watch out. Make sure you don't use *it* to refer to different things, especially within a single paragraph.

The same thing goes for *they, them*, and *their*, as well as *he* and *his,* and *she* and *her.*

Generally speaking, reducing your reliance on "it" (and other imprecise pronouns) will make for richer writing (and reading). Strive for clarity without redundancy.

One of the most common misspellings is using *its* when you mean *it's*. Its, not it's, is the possessive form of "it." It's = it is.

Here's an ugly sentence from the corporate website of Sir Speedy, which is a national printing franchise:

Its not easy being creative and we know that.

But it *is* easy to be sloppy.

## Italics.

Italics are used for the names of ships, planes, and trains; internal thoughts; titles of record albums, movies, and books; titles of newspapers and magazines; foreign words and phrases that have not been commonly accepted into general use (and, in some cases, never will); the Latin names of plants and animals; and legal cases.

Capitalizing restaurant names, businesses, and company names is enough: no italics are needed.

**Important note #1:** Be sure to encompass *all* letters and symbols in an italicized word or phrase: it's very easy to leave out the first or last letter or symbol, and difficult to see when you do.

**Important note #2: DO NOT DO NOT DO NOT** use bold for emphasis in a college paper. It's just not done.

**Italics and book titles.**

If the title of a book is long, it is entirely appropriate to reduce the length in a way that will still make your readers understand immediately which book you are talking about. A good rule of thumb is to use the entire title from time to time, perhaps at the beginning of each chapter or on a regular, consistent basis to refresh your readers' memories.

For example, say you regularly refer to *The Pocket Guide to Brunswick, Maine with two maps.* If you simply wrote the pocket guide within the text, the significance of the words "the pocket guide" would disappear and likely confuse your readers. The Pocket Guide would not be correct, since it would not indicate that the words represent the title of a book. Use *The Pocket Guide.*

Example: *The Complete Biography Workbook with two templates* can be shortened to *The Workbook.*

**Italics and newspaper titles.**

According to *The Associated Press Stylebook (AP)*, when writing the titles of newspapers, you should italicize and capitalize the word *the* when it is part of the title. It's best to look at the newspaper's website to determine its exact title and italicize accordingly.

If you need to add the city or state to the title, like the *Portland* [Maine] *Press Herald*, put the additional information in brackets. Authorities are divided about whether to italicize the additional information; since it is not part of the title, it is a little difficult to justify italicizing it.

**Italics and ships, planes, and trains.**

Examples: "Oh, how wonderful!" she said. "Dear me, I can quite see you. The *Golden Hind*! Spanish treasure! All that pomp and majesty!"

We'll take the *Orient Express* to Istanbul.

(Note: some style manuals do not suggest italicizing the names of trains.)

The *Enola Gay* delivered the atomic bomb, code-named "Little Boy," to Hiroshima, Japan.

Do not italicize the USS, HMS or RMS portion of a ship's name. It's the RMS *Titanic*, the HMS *Invincible*, and the USS *Wasp*.

Do not italicize the make or model of a vehicle: Alfa Romeo Spyder, Lamborghini Diablo Roadster VT, Cadillac deVille convertible, BMW 545i.

**Italics and plurals and the possessive.**

If a word is italicized, like the name of a submarine, the -s or -es that forms the plural is *not* italicized.

Examples: *Sturgeon*s, *Permit*s, and Los *Angeles*es

Same thing with the possessive: the *Porgy*'s.

**Italics and foreign words.**

Italics are appropriate when using a foreign word or phrase that has not reached a point of being commonly known and used in America.

For example, menu and cachet are both words that, once upon a time, would have been italicized, but now neither of them has to be set off by italics, since these words are in common usage.

If you use a foreign word or phrase that will probably not be understood by your readers, you may put the translation in parenthesis next to the word or phrase.

Words and phrases that have not become part of an everyday vocabulary, however, like *schadenfreude, deus ex machina, sui generis,* and *sine qua non,* should be italicized.

Examples:

Her bed was paved with hats; it was a *parterre* of hats, of which the boxes stood on the floor, a rampart of boxes.

He was the professional *jeune premier* in social circles at Tilling, smart and beautifully dressed and going to more tea parties than anybody else, and it was not at all amiss that he should imperil his reputation and hers by these gay audacities.

To change "example" gears entirely:

Default affidavits are a lender's representation as to the status of a loan. They are routinely accepted in both state and federal courts *in lieu* of live testimony.

Also, foreign phrases that begin with "a" or *de* probably should be italicized, simply so your readers don't stumble.

Example: Robert Quantock, the wag who had danced a hornpipe when Georgie had appeared in the original voluminousness, was waggish again, when he saw the abbreviated garments, and *à propos* of nothing in particular, had said, "Home is the sailor, home from the sea," and that was the epitaph on the Oxford trousers.

(See the Accents and Symbols section to learn how to create accents in Microsoft Word.)

**Italics and thoughts.**

When a character is thinking, using italics for his or her thoughts is a very easy way to convey that fact to your readers.

If you want to emphasize a word or phrase while using italics, standardize the font of that word or phrase.

Example: *I wish I had the nerve to wear* that *one*, Liz thought, as she admired the low-cut red dress.

**Important note.** In conversation, one character could have "thoughts" (as in an opinion) that that person expresses out loud; in other words, you can imagine someone saying to someone else, "Well, my mother thinks we should bake the tangerine-pecan pie for Christmas because that's her favorite." However, you will confuse your readers if, in a conversation in your work, you write something like this:

"Mom, do you have an opinion?" I asked.

"I can make my key lime pie," Lisa volunteered eagerly.

"I would rather have the tangerine-pecan pie for Christmas dinner," my mother thought. "It seems more Christmas-y, somehow."

"Okay. Tangerine-pecan it is. One or two?"

Don't use "thought" as a substitute for "said" or a similar equivalent to express a character's spoken conversation; save the "thoughts" for unexpressed ideas or mental activity.

## Italics vs. Quotation Marks.

Italics can be used for emphasis. Quotation marks are appropriate when you are talking about a word as a "word," when you (or one of your characters) would likely use your index and middle fingers to create the "quote-unquote" gesture. Sometimes, when someone has a longish list of words he or she is talking about, then using italics and not quotation marks looks cleaner.

I had a tough time deciding whether or not to italicize a when I was discussing the letter a or whether to put the a in quotation marks: "a." I finally decided—in general—to use quotation marks when referring to single letters, since italicized single letters are so difficult to see, and to use italics when referring to words of more than one letter.

Take a look at these two examples.

Commas are used to separate main clauses joined by *and, but, or, nor*, or *for.*

Commas are used to separate main clauses joined by "and," "but," "or," "nor," or "for."

The first sentence is cleaner visually, while still being clear.

Example: The letter a is an indefinite article.

Example: The letter “a” is an indefinite article.

Example: The letter *a* is an indefinite article.

In the first sentence, without the a being set off somehow, is difficult to read. The second sentence makes the “a” special enough to be readily recognized, while the italicized *a* in the last sentence pretty much disappears.

## The “Rule of Pie.”

Have you ever wondered when to use quotation marks or italics? Ha! This is a cool rule. Think about a pie. The totality of the pie—the title of the book, the record album name, the name of the newspaper—are all placed in italics. The pieces of the pie—the name of the poem, the song title, the article—are all placed in quotation marks. Is that cool, or what? I do not want to brag (perish the thought), but I’m pretty sure I made that up, all by myself.

### Italics for emphasis.

Italics can be used for emphasis, but should be used sparingly.

Example: “But it wouldn’t be *that* sort of party,” said Georgie.

Italics can indicate a loud sound, though this is not necessary.

Example: There was an enormous *boom*, and everyone scrambled for cover.

### Emphasis in an *italicized* sentence.

Okay, we understand that italics are used to emphasize content. Sometimes it is used stylistically; for example, an entire passage could be italicized, to distinguish that passage from other writing in another font displayed on the same page. We know that to emphasize a word in an italicized sentence we go back to the regular, unitalicized font. Take a look at this last sentence in a long blog post about building a fan base. The writer is trying to sell me software that he says will improve my ability to build a fan base:

*What do you do with your content to build your fan* base?

The entire sentence is italicized except for the word "base." Why is "base" emphasized? He's built me up to a fever pitch and now comes the hook, the fear created by the blog, the question he wants me to ask myself: What *am* I doing to build a fan base????

The word that should be italicized is *your.*

What a *wasted* opportunity.

**Using italics in the Latin names of plants and animals.**

Italics are used when quoting the Latin name of plants and animals. Capitalize the genus, lowercase the species. *The New York Times'* style guide specifies using Times New Roman as the font, though that seems a little precious.

Examples: *Hydrangea macrophylla, Ilex* 'Nellie R. Stevens,' *Homo sapiens, Felis catus, Canis lupus familiaris.*

In a sentence: The *Homo sapiens* planted the *Ilex* 'Nellie R. Stevens' while the *Felis catus* and the *Canis lupus familiaris* watched.

Note the use of single quotes in this instance.

**Use italics when quoting court cases.**

A few months prior to this Court's finding, in *In re Fagan*, Case No. 04-23460, the United States Bankruptcy Court for the Southern District of New York made a virtually identical finding. The practice of underlining court cases is passé (which I found out *after* I wrote my 67-page petition to the 2nd DCA). By the way, in court cases, "re" is pronounced "ray."

**Italics can indicate response.**

In a church program, the clergy's spoken part is generally in a standard font, while the congregation's response is in italics. ("Bolding" can also be used for the same purpose.)

Example:

Celebrant: Blessed be God: Father, Son, and Holy Ghost.

People: *And blessed be his kingdom, now and for ever. Amen.*

**Italics don'ts.**

Do not italicize the titles of sacred works: the Bible, the Torah, and the Quran. Note: adjectives and adverbs derived from the titles of sacred works —biblically, biblical, and so on—are not capitalized.

Do not combine italics and quotation marks for a character's thoughts. If you want to provide emphasis in a thought, revert to the standard font.

Consider this example:

Green? *That's what he meant by* green? she thought. *He's crazy!*

That example emphasized the word *green.* Here's the same sentence, with the emphasis on *crazy*:

*Green? That's what he meant by green?* she thought. *He's* crazy*!*

By changing the italicized word, the focus of the entire sentence changes.

## Test your knowledge!

What's wrong with these sentences? (Answers follow.)

1. No jeans, no flip flops, no t-shirts, no tank tops.
2. Each academy member will have the opportunity to deliver a 3-5 minute signature story or portion of a speech and be recorded.

3. Founded in 2005, our organization offers frequent educational and social events, mentoring and an user-generated, dynamic Web site where interactive professionals can connect, collaborate, network and learn.

4. Since we founded the company in 2011, Signet is driven by personal initiative and commitment to going further for our Clients.

5. You have to meet your audience where they congregate.

6. From there, we execute using our proven processes of development, content creativity, quality assurance, and publishing that consistently generates focused results.

7. If you are interested in purchasing multiple pairs using different prescriptions (e.g. one for you and one for your spouse; one pair for distance and one for reading), please place a separate order for each prescription.

8. But this group, the Great Enlightened Society of Oculists, was devoted to more than just opthalmology, and their advancements were not limited to medical techniques alone: noblemen and merchants alike were allowed to join, as were women.

9. Instead, imagine how the Wall St. Journal or Forbes magazine might describe what you do to their readers.

10. By the mid 1970's, requests had begun to come from all over the country for Boar's Head products.

11. Your Clients can log-in to your website

12. I arrive 90 minutes before my equipment needs to be setup. My actual setup takes about thirty minutes.

13. We intent to keep the original look and feel of our website while refreshing some aspects of the site.

**Answers:**

1. "T-shirts" needs a capital T: No jeans, no flip flops, no T-shirts, no tank tops.

2. Here we have the suspended hyphen rule. The sentence should have been written:

Each academy member will have the opportunity to deliver a 3- to 5-minute signature story or portion of a speech and be recorded.

3. Big mistake here: what's *an* doing in front of *user*? Plus, I would argue that it's *website*, not *Web site*. I'd add a one-word elaboration about the mentoring. And, I'd add a comma after *where* and two serial commas. The sentence should read: Founded in 2005, our organization offers frequent educational and social events, effective mentoring, and a user-generated, dynamic website, where interactive professionals can connect, collaborate, network, and learn.

4. There's a problem with the verb agreement, since *founded* should be matched with *has been driven* and *to go*. And why is clients capitalized? Here's the corrected version:

Since the company was founded in 2011, Signet has been driven by personal initiative and commitment to go further for our clients. (Using *our* is acceptable here; *its* would have okay also.)

5. Oh, no you don't! *Audience* is a *collective* noun, which means it is a *singular* noun, which means this sentence could be written in two ways:

You have to meet your audience where it congregates.

You have to meet your audience members where they congregate.

6. *Processes* is plural; *generates* is singular. This from a company that is touting its publishing prowess! Here's the sentence, minus that all-important "s": From there, we execute, using our proven processes of development, content creativity, quality assurance, and publishing that consistently generate focused results.

7. Where's the comma after e.g.?

8. This sentence has serious problems, the most important of which—it's an eyeglass site—is the misspelling of *ophthalmology*. But there's also the issue of collective noun-pronoun agreement, with *group* and *their*. Corrected, it reads: But this group, the Great Enlightened Society of Oculists, was devoted to more than just ophthalmology, and its advancements were not limited to medical techniques alone: noblemen and merchants alike were allowed to join, as were women.

9. I can practically guarantee you that if you write like this, neither *The Wall Street Journal* nor *Forbes* will *ever* describe what it is that you do to

*anybody!* Go to The Wall Street Journal's website to find out how it styles itself: it's *The Wall Street Journal*, not Wall St. Journal. Always italicize newspaper and magazine titles. Plus, *or* is not *and*: nouns joined by *or* agree in quantity with the noun closest to *or*, which would make the pronoun...singular. So: Instead, imagine how *The Wall Street Journal* or *Forbes* magazine might describe what you do to its readers. (I think I'd suggest *and* as the conjunction, not *or*.)

10. The problem with this sentence is with the date, which should read mid-1970s.

11. This sentence was from a site that writes website content (for money!) and was one of many, many, many problematic sentences in *its* content. Why is "Clients" capitalized? And, no hyphen in "log in" as a compound verb. Corrected, the sentence reads: Your clients can log in to your website.

12. In this situation, *set up*, used as a verb, should be *two* words: I arrive 90 minutes before my equipment needs to be set up. The next sentence, when *setup* is used as a noun, is correct. Read the two sentences out loud and listen to the difference. As a noun: one word. As a verb: two words.

13. Gee, I think *intend* was what was intended here, don't you?

We intend to keep the original look and feel of our website while refreshing some aspects of the site.

Let's hope one of the things that they refreshed was their content!

## Me, myself, and I.

In traditional grammar, "I" is used only as a subject, *me* is used only as an object, and *myself* is used only as a reflexive object, when the subject is "I" and the object would otherwise be *me*. *Myself* is often used incorrectly, and should only be used when the speaker is both the subject and object of the verb, or as an emphatic pronoun.

Here are some examples:

Standard: Liz and I took the bus.

(Not "Liz and me took the bus." You wouldn't say "Me took the bus.")

Standard: She gave the cookies to Liz and me.

(Not "She gave the cookies to Liz and I." You wouldn't say "She gave the cookies to I.")

Acceptable, if stiff: That is I in the photo.

Acceptable: That is me in the photo. (This is typical in informal, spoken English.)

Standard (intensifying): I myself have witnessed acts of kindness between strangers.

Standard (reflexive): I went to the movie by myself.

Nonstandard: Liz and me went into the bar.

(Correct: Liz and I went into the bar. I went into the bar. Liz went into the bar. We went into the bar.)

Nonstandard: Me and Liz went into the bar. (You'd never say "Me went into the bar.")

Nonstandard: As for myself, I like the beach. (As for me, I like the beach.)

Nonstandard: She gave the cookies to Liz and myself. (She gave the cookies to Liz and me.)

## Names.

Capitalize first, middle, and last names.

If someone prefers to use an initial or initials, put a period after the initial and a space.

Example: E. H. Coursen

If, however, someone is known by his or her initials, do not use a period or a space between the letters.

Example: JB, LBJ, MLK, JFK

Note: some style manuals do not use a comma between a man's name and "junior," e.g., Paul B. Mason Junior.

If a name is preceded by *de, du, d', de la, von,* etc.—these are called particles—use the spelling most commonly used. Always capitalize particles at the beginning of a sentence.

Examples:

Claus von Bulöw was accused of murdering his wife.

Von Bulöw was accused of attempted murder.

**Hyphenated names must include both elements.**

Example: Mrs. Mapp-Flint, she yelled, had polled eight hundred and five votes, and was therefore elected.

Conveying hyphenated ancestry is complicated and there is no agreement between prevailing authorities: *Chicago* says no hyphens and so does Princeton; *AP* says that some "dual heritage" nouns get one (Italian- and Mexican-American are examples), but some don't (examples given are French Canadian and Latin American). We all know that the construct Native American does not have a hyphen. Other style guides say no hyphens as stand-alone nouns, but *yes* to hyphens when modifying another noun. Every time it seems as though a rule can be established (no hyphens when it is region + American), an exception pops up that knocks the rule down.

This is wishy washy. No hyphens. Ever. I agree with *Chicago*: "the hyphen does not aid comprehension." I am for clarity and continuity, and I say *no* to hyphens.

**Nicknames can be written several ways.**

Examples:

Elizabeth "Liz" Huntoon Coursen

Liz Coursen

Elizabeth (Liz) Huntoon Coursen

Elizabeth Huntoon Coursen (Liz)

Note: If you are planning to refer to the person by his or her nickname later in your text, the second example of these two that follows is the best choice for the first use of the name:

Charles Augustus Lindbergh, "Lucky Lindy"

Douglas "Wrong Way" Corrigan

**When a title appears before a person's name, capitalize it.**

Example: By curious coincidence, she met Major Benjy on the threshold.

If the title follows a person's name, do not capitalize it.

Example: Liz Coursen used to be the director of the marketing department.

**If a title stands in for a character, feel free to capitalize the title.**

Example: "And further to come down yet," said the Padre, "for they had another drink together, and the poor Major's mind must have got in a fair jumble."

## Animals and pronouns.

According to *The New York Times,* if an animal is named and its sex can be determined by its name, or is known, a writer can refer to the animal as "he" or "she." So, you would call a great white shark that is a known male a "he," you would call your dog, Annie, a "she," but a random squirrel in your backyard or a stray cat is an "it." I would still use "that," instead of "who" though: the dog "that" did...whatever.

## Numbers, dates, and times.

### Numbers.

Use hyphens with numbers that are definite: scores, times, distances, telephone numbers, Social Security numbers. Use dashes to indicate a range.

When numbers occur frequently in everything but a technical paper, the established practice is to spell out numbers from one to ten, and to use figures (11, 12, etc.) for all others.

When numbers are not used often, authors typically spell out all numbers that can be expressed in one or two words and use figures for others.

Try not to begin a sentence with a number. If you must, spell it out.

Example: Nineteen cats is eighteen too many.

The only exception is starting a sentence with a year:

2008 was a difficult year for me.

Note: When starting a sentence with a number and unit, both must be spelled out as words. (Again, this is something to avoid if possible.)

Example: Three o'clock in the morning is a tough time to do any meaningful studying.

Note: I edited a manuscript recently where the author used many dates from the 1700s and 1800s. Right in the middle of the text she said that a shipbuilder had built 1775 boats, meaning one thousand, seven hundred, and seventy-five. I put a comma in the number (1,775) to lessen number versus date confusion.

**Numbers in sports.**

You will almost always use figures, not words, for sports-related numbers, from yardage gained or lost, to the winning time of a 50-meter relay, to the final score.

## Ages.

For ages, most style manuals suggest using figures, as opposed to words. If the age is used as an adjective or as a substitute for a noun, then it should be hyphenated. Don't use apostrophes when describing an age range.

Examples:

A fifty-two-year-old author. A 52-year-old author. The author is 52 years old.

The girl, 11, had a sister who was 14.

The contest is for 12-year-olds.

He is in his 40s. (Remember: the plural of all numbers is formed by adding "s" to the number.)

## Dimensions and distances.

When writing about height, distance, or other dimensions, use figures and spell out words such as feet, miles, etc. If you do use symbols, there is no space between a number and the symbols for dollars, feet, inches, degrees, or percent.

Don't forget: inches and feet do not use quotation marks or apostrophes, they use prime and double prime marks, which are simply nondirectional apostrophes (one for inches, two for feet). Because prime marks are not quotation marks, the period is placed outside the prime marks if these come at the end of a sentence.

Examples:

She is 5-foot-3. Or, she is five-three. Or, she is five feet, three inches tall. Or, she is 5' 2".

He wrote with a 2-inch pencil.

The driveway is 25 feet long. (25 feet is *after* the noun it modifies.)

I'd hate to have to plow a 5-mile-long driveway.

The industry standard for purchasing lumber is thickness by (represented by a lowercase "x") width; length will vary. Even though the *AP Stylebook* prefers that everything be spelled out with hyphens (two-by-four), that is not necessary for clarity; 2 in. x 4 in. is acceptable, as is 2 x 4s when talking about multiple pieces:

I need ten 2 x 4s. (2 [space] x [lowercase] space 4 [no space with "s" (if plural)

The paper was 8.5-by-11 inches. (Though 8.5"-by-11" or 8.5"x11" would also be correct.)

The monitor's resolution was 1280 x 1024. (Not 1280 by 1024.)

**When comparing the metric system and U.S. "customary units."**

Note: if you must offer your readers a side-by-side comparison of metric system units and U.S. measurements, the cleanest way to display the information is like this:

I walked X miles (X kilometers) to the village.

Another way that results in a "cleaner" text is to add a table at some convenient place in your text, so readers can refer to it as necessary, especially if you are writing for an American audience.

## Temperature and angles.

To write the degree symbol in Microsoft Word, turn on your Number Lock, hold down Alt, and type 0176 on the number keys to the far right of your keyboard. There is no space between the number and the degree symbol.

Example: 90°

## pH.

The proper method of reporting pH is to place the unit before the number (pH 4); do put a space between the pH and the number, but never insert the word *of* between the unit and number—they should always go together.

## Money.

You can handle money in two ways, either by using a symbol coupled with the amount in figures, or by spelling out the amount and adding the words "dollars" or "cents" or whatever. If you choose to represent money with the symbol plus the figure, use decimal points and commas where appropriate.

Do not write $ + amount + "dollars." It's either $ + amount or amount + "dollars," but not both. $14 million dollars, for example, is incorrect because you have both a dollar sign and the word "dollars" together, which is redundant. (No space between the $ sign and the number.)

Example: If you publish a thesis that's 400 pages long, using a good-quality paper, the cost per page should be somewhere around four cents per page, so you're looking at right around $16 just for the copying.

Or: When I looked in my pocket, I discovered I had twenty-two dollars in all —not nearly enough.

When you want to convey a range of money, like $1 million up to $2 million, either use a dash—which conveys a range—or write $1 million to $2 million, not $1 to $2 million.

Note: Like with time, when you don't have to add :00 if you are speaking about the top of the hour, you don't have to add .00 if the amount contains no cents.

## Fractions.

For numbers smaller than one, write out the fraction, and use a hyphen between the words.

Examples: one-half, two-thirds of an inch

## Percentages.

Write out *percent*, unless you are writing a technical paper or manual. If you do use the % symbol, there is no space: 50%.

Example: I generally sell my book to 50 percent of an audience.

If, as above, the object of the preposition, the "of" part, refers to a singular word, *percent* takes a singular verb. If, however, the "of" construction refers to a plural noun, you use a plural verb:

Liz found that fully 70 percent of the web pages she reviewed were rife with errors.

Use a hyphen between the number and *percent* when they are used as a compound adjective and precede the modified noun. (Note: *The Chicago Manual of Style* states that there should never be a hyphen between a number and the word *percent* at any time; *AP* is silent on this specific issue, and other authorities disagree with *Chicago*, but, to my mind, the hyphen makes sense.)

Example: My sales figures show a 50-percent increase since last year, which is very encouraging.

Remember the lesson about suspended hyphens:

I hope to achieve a 40- to 50-percent increase in sales this year compared to last year.

## Model numbers.

Always use figures to represent a model number or product name.

Example: I loved my BMW 545i: it was fast as hell.

## Dates.

Use an apostrophe before figures expressing a decade if numerals are left out: the '90s, or, the Nineties. Make sure the apostrophe faces "out" or "away" from the number, which indicates that what's missing is in front of what's there.

Use the letter "s" with no apostrophe after figures when expressing decades.

Example: the 1900s

Generally, spell out the century. It's either "the twelfth century" or, when used as a compound adjective, "a twelfth-century painting."

Always spell out the month when referring to a specific date. When the full date is within a sentence, use a comma after the day and after the year.

Example: As of January 1, 2014, my tenant had six cats.

When using the date as an adjective, do not use a comma after the year.

Example: The December 2, 2010 tournament was rained out.

When writing the month and the year but no day, do not use a comma between the month and the year.

Example: In August 2011, Miss Coursen had 17 book tour events, including seven in the metro-Miami area.

Note: In general, it is not necessary to include a *–nd*, *-rd*, or *–st* following a number. For example, January 1 (as opposed to January 1st) conveys exactly what you want your readers to know, even though when you write "January 15," you likely say "January fifteenth."

## Times.

Specify as necessary: a.m. and p.m. or AM and PM—no spaces—are acceptable, but be consistent. (Of the two, the lowercase version is perhaps more common.) Sometimes an author will use capitals, though in a slightly smaller font, which is also acceptable. If a.m. or p.m. ends a sentence, that period serves as the period for the sentence.

The precise time when an event has occurred or will occur is unnecessary for most stories. Of course, there are occasions when the time of day is important. In such cases, use figures, but spell out noon and midnight. Do not write 12 noon or 12 midnight (it's redundant). Use a colon to separate hours from minutes, but do not use :00. There's a space between the number and a.m./p.m.

Examples: 1 p.m., 3:30 a.m., 4 o'clock, 11 AM

When referring to military time, it is acceptable to write "We left at 0630."

To distinguish between the time of day within sections of the country, though there is disagreement among style experts (*Chicago* says no caps, except for "Pacific," while *AP* says first-letter caps), it does make sense to capitalize all words associated with a specific time, e.g., Eastern Daylight Time, Daylight Saving Time, Central Standard Time, and so on. The abbreviations should be all capitals, with no periods: EST, DST, CST, etc.

Note: Adding an "s" at the end of "s" at the end of Saving in Daylight Saving Time is becoming increasingly common, especially in spoken English, just as an "s" is becoming common with words like *towards,* and is probably because it makes the words flow more easily in conversation. In written English, however, Daylight Savings Time is incorrect.

In conversation, it is acceptable to not use all the words that follow the initial designation.

Example: "Eight-forty Eastern," she said.

## Let's test your knowledge!

Is there anything wrong with these sentences? (Answers follow.)

1. Much like the unicorn with the golden horn or the hairy beast named Bigfoot, you may have thought the redheaded, freckle-faced stepchild was a myth.

Chapter 1. Punctuation and Grammar.

2. The educational summit, now in it's seventh year, explores current trends and best practices in marketing, design, user experience and strategy in an environment that inspires creativity and learning.

3. Mr. Stone graduated from the University of Wisconsin, Madison, with Honours, with a Bachelors of Business Administration degree in Finance.

4. Dog adoption fees start at just $55 - a small price to pay for a wonderful companion!

5. But, our standards for quality have never waved - a value passed down from one family member to the next.

6. Main Line Family Law Center is a husband and wife team on a mission to help couples through their separation and divorce as seamless and painless as possible.

7. Everybody — salespeople, marketers, customer and prospects — have been impressed with the our website.

8. If a job you've accepted has an Editor Review stage, the content will be reveiwed by an editor who has been hired by the client or agency.

9. If the best writers don't take your offer, we will gradually bid up the price offer - up to your max price... ensuring you get the highest rated writer, at the lowest possible price.

10. ""The only way to win at content marketing is for the reader to say, 'This was written specifically for me."

11. Jim Jackson is President and Chief Executive Officer of Northeastern Bank in Sarasota and Manatee Counties.

12. Although many events involve less than 100 attendees, automating administrative functions for simple events results in significant cost savings, conservation of staff time and the opportunity to focus resources on higher level tasks.

13. I think reducing sugar intake is a fantastic idea, reducing sugar and salt at the same time is even better and yields results in other aspects of health that compliment each other.

14. I read the *New York Times*, the *Washington Post*, and CNN everyday.

**Answers:**

1. Nothing is wrong with this sentence. The rule about hyphenating two words that end in *-ed* is to drop the *-ed* in the first word, which the author did. Things got complicated with the introduction of "redheaded," but that just made the sentence complicated, not incorrect.

2. Oops! This sentence is from the homepage of a big-city marketing group, and contains the most basic of punctuation mistakes: the infamous *it's* for *its* mistake. Ouch! The corrected sentence would read: The educational summit, now in its seventh year, explores current trends and best practices in marketing, design, user experience and strategy in an environment that inspires creativity and learning.

3. Well, let's see. I'd suggest hyphenating the place from which the degree was received; *Bachelor's* needs an apostrophe; and, last time I looked, Wisconsin is in America, so *Honours* should be spelled in its American version: Mr. Stone graduated from the University of Wisconsin-Madison, with Honors, with a Bachelor's of Business Administration degree in Finance.

Or, better: Mr. Stone received his Bachelor's of Business Administration in Finance, with Honors, from the University of Wisconsin-Madison.

4. That's a hyphen, and the sentence needs a *dash.*

5. This is a cringe-worthy sentence. First off, standards might be *waived*, and standards can *waver*, but they sure aren't *waved*. Secondly, that's a hyphen (with spaces!), and what the sentence needs a dash.

6. Here's another really ugly sentence. First off, two people can't *be* a business. They can *own* a business, they can *run* a business, they can *staff* a business, but they can't *be* a business, so something has to be added here. Hyphens are needed between husband-and-wife because the phrase is a compound adjective that appears before the noun it modifies. And then there's the mess at the end: as seamless*ly* and painless*ly* as possible is correct. Here's what you end up with:

Main Line Family Law Center is owned by a husband-and-wife team on a mission to help couples through their separation and divorce as seamlessly and painlessly as possible.

7. Well, aside from the no-spaces-before-and-after-the-dash rule (we're against them), we've got a serious problem with noun-verb agreement, since "everybody" is singular, and so the verb should have been "has." And, then, then there's the issue of the obvious fact that no one bothered to edit this sentence. If you missed the major problem, read it again....

8. If you can ignore that nasty misspelled word, all is well in this sentence from a company that hires writers to write online content. The company's content is simply stuffed with mistakes and typos. Wow, wow, and wow.

9. Oh, heck, why not another sentence from this same site? Pretty soon, I'll have to give it attribution! Let's see, there's a hyphen (with spaces) and it needs a dash, and then there's the three-point ellipsis with a space, and there shouldn't be a space at all.

10. Yes, this is from the same site. I can't help myself. And it is pretty obvious that there's a problem with quotation marks in this sentence, which is an actual quote. The rule is double quotes around what the person speaking is actually saying, and single quotes around what the speaker is quoting. But, it's a little worse than just that mistake because there are actually two types of quotation marks in this single sentence: a "smart" pair and a nondirectional pair. Yikes. Here it is, corrected: "The only way to win at content marketing is for the reader to say, 'This was written specifically for me.'"

Note: sometimes a writer will chose to put a space between single and double quotes, especially when the quotation marks nestle against one another. That's fine, just be consistent.

11. This is a capitalization-problem sentence. Because Mr. Jackson's titles follow his name, they should not be capitalized. Plus, *counties* should not be capitalized.

12. Read the definition of *fewer* and *less* in the "Commonly Misspelled/Misused Words" section at the end of Chapter 2 to see that "less" is used incorrectly in this sentence. Plus, I'd want a serial comma after "staff time," and I'd hyphenate higher-level. So, this sentence should read: Although many events involve fewer than 100 attendees, automating administrative functions for simple events results in significant cost savings, conservation of staff time, and the opportunity to focus resources on higher-level tasks.

13. Yuck! There's the comma splice for one, and the word *compliment* is misspelled: in this use, it's *complement* (to complete). Sloppy!

14. Both the "thes" in front of the newspaper titles should be capitalized and italicized, and "everyday" should be "every day."

## Parentheses.

Style note: Use parentheses sparingly and appropriately.

Parentheses are used to emphasize content. They place more emphasis on the enclosed content than commas, but less than dashes. Like commas when used to create parenthetical information and dashes, though, used properly you can "pull" the entirety of the contents of the parentheses out of your sentence and the sentence will still make sense. Unlike commas and dashes, however, parentheses *always* come in pairs.

Authors typically use parentheses to draw attention away from the action, using the parentheses to add information that only the author would know, as a sort of aside. Oftentimes, parentheses seem to be a message directly from the author (or a character) him- or herself.

Example: "And is your ladyship making a long stay in Tilling?" asked the (real) Major, to cover the pause which had been caused by Mr. Wyse saying something across the table to Isabel.

A great example of an aside during a storytelling, from *Watership Down*:

> "The next day in the afternoon, it began to rain.
> ("Those scrapes we dug in the bank," whispered Buckthorn to Dandelion.)

More examples, this time from Stephen King's thrilling *Fire-Starter*:

He had no illusions about his looks or his line, which were both pretty nondescript, or about the girl's probable status (pinned or engaged), but it was a nice day, and he was feeling good.

Parentheses are distinguished from dashes in that their content is a little more removed from the subject matter at hand, while dashes indicate a sharper break in thought or action, but the information contained within the dashes has more of a direct bearing on the action.

Consider these two examples, one using parentheses and the other using dashes:

He looked rather worried, she thought (as well he might), and passing on he disappeared round the church corner, clearly on his way to his betrothed.

There were Susan's sables there—it was thoughtful of Susan, but ostentatious—and there was a carriage rug, which she was convinced was new, and was very likely a present from Mr. Wyse.

Parentheses serve to give the reader additional information as an aside.

Examples:

She had made up her mind about the laundry; she intended to pay that bill with an icy countenance and say "Good morning for ever," or words to that effect, unless the proprietor instantly produced the—the article of clothing which had been lost in the wash (like King John's treasures), or refunded an ample sum for the replacing of it.

Lucia used her highest art in making a copy (on Mallards paper) of this document, as if writing hastily in a familiar medium.

Figgis brought in a note on an immense silver (probably plated) salver and presented it to the Contessa; it was to be delivered at once.

**Punctuation inside parentheses.**

In American English, it is not desirable to create a complete sentence *inside* a complete sentence. If the parenthetical information is inside another sentence, here are the rules:

If the parenthetical information is in the middle of the sentence, the first letter of the first word (except for proper nouns and *I*) inside the parenthesis is not capitalized. No period, either, even if there is a complete sentence inside the parentheses, but do use an exclamation point or question mark if that's what's required. A comma, if necessary, is always placed after (outside) the second parenthesis.

An example, from Richard Adams' terrific classic *Watership Down*:

Rabbits (says Mr. Lockley) are like human beings in many ways.

Here are several examples from *Fire-Starter*:

> Andy left the lecture hall, started across the lobby toward the big double doors (outside, the quad was green with approaching summer, students passing desultorily back and forth), and then remembered his pen.
>
> OJ's report was nearly unbelievable: they had known the girl had *something*, but this story of sudden carnage and reversal was (at least to Cap) like a bolt of lightning from a clear blue sky.
>
> Rammaden, who had died three years ago (Rainbird had sent flowers to his funeral—what a comedy life could sometimes be!), had taught them about...
>
> In many ways she felt that the last five months (they told her it was five months; it didn't feel like anything) had been a dream.

If the parenthetical information is composed of two sentences, put the appropriate end punctuation after the first sentence, and then capitalize the first word of the second sentence and use appropriate end punctuation at the end of *that* sentence.

Example: The rules of punctuation (surprise! There are rules!) are easy to learn, but difficult to master.

If the parenthetical information is a complete sentence and comes at the end of the sentence, then put an exclamation point or a question mark if necessary (but never a period) immediately inside the second parenthesis, with a period outside: punctuation mark + parenthesis + period. This is an awkward-looking construction, and you might want to rewrite to avoid it.

Again from *Fire-Starter*:

> He told Andy that Rainbird was a Shop hitter who had been horribly wounded in Vietnam, had lost an eye there (the one-eyed pirate in my dream, Andy thought numbly).
>
> He had come at quarter to five, half an hour ago, and had introduced himself as Captain Hollister ("but please just call me Cap; everyone does").

If the parenthetical information constitutes a stand-alone sentence, then you'll punctuate the entire sentence inside the parentheses: first letter capitalized, punctuation mark at the end—the whole nine yards—like this passage from *Watership Down*:

"Fine. Fine. Good fellas. Plenty beetle." (All insects were "beetle" to Kehaar.)

Punctuating information enclosed by parentheses is not the same as punctuating using commas or dashes.

Consider this sentence:

He ought to know, for Christmas (as usual in December) was daily drawing nearer...

Had the "as usual in December" phrase been enclosed by commas, there would be a comma after "Christmas" and another after "December."

Had dashes been used, their placement would have been the same as the pair of commas:

He ought to know, for Christmas—as usual in December—was daily drawing nearer...

Basically, what's happening here is the first parenthesis takes the place of the first comma or dash, but a comma is still necessary after the second parenthesis.

Here's another example of when a comma was necessary after the parenthetical information.

Original text: And only last week, being plucked from slumber by some unaccountable indigestion (for which she blamed a small green apple), she had seen at no less than twelve thirty in the morning the lights in Captain Puffin's sitting room still shining through the blind.

The information about the apple is presented as an aside; it is information not at all necessary to the action at hand.

Here's the same sentence punctuated with commas:

And only last week, being plucked from slumber by some unaccountable indigestion, for which she blamed a small green apple, she had seen at no less than twelve thirty in the morning the lights in Captain Puffin's sitting room still shining through the blind.

Though technically correct, the information about the source of the indigestion is presented as a more important part of the action than it really deserves to be.

Compare this same sentence punctuated with dashes:

And only last week, being plucked from slumber by some unaccountable indigestion—for which she blamed a small green apple—she had seen at no less than twelve thirty in the morning the lights in Captain Puffin's sitting room still shining through the blind.

Now the information about the apple is front and center—it was an *apple* that caused Miss Mapp's indigestion!—and the result of the dashes is that the apple is catapulted into the forefront of the action. With the information about the apple set off by dashes, the reader would expect much more information about apples, orchards, and indigestion to be included to make such an emphasis logical; since there is no other apple-related (or digestion-related) information included, setting off the apple information with dashes does not make sense.

Note: these sentences are all from E. F. Benson's *Make Way for Lucia*. Mr. Benson is known for his use of humor and irony, and most of his more obvious humorous asides are set off by dashes or parentheses, depending on the circumstances. Sometimes it's a real draw whether a dash or parentheses was best.

Example: Only a foolish, ingenuous child (and Elizabeth was anything but that) could have considered these as isolated phenomena.

After reading that sentence with the original parentheses, you could really make a case for dashes as well.

Use parentheses to set off nonessential material, such as dates or sources, from a sentence.

Muhammad Ali (1942-2016), arguably one of the greatest athletes of all time, claimed he could "float like a butterfly, sting like a bee."

**Parentheses caution:** Parentheses should be used sparingly. There are only so many times you speak to your reader *sotto voce.*

## Plurals.

Plurals can be tricky. For example, the preferred plural of "salvo" is "salvos," though "salvoes" is acceptable. The plural of "flamingo" is listed in the dictionary as either "flamingoes" or "flamingos," while the plurals of both tomato and potato are both made by adding *–es*, with no option for adding the "s" by itself.

Then, of course, there are the many words whose plural forms are not created by adding "s" or *–es*: foot/feet, child/children, mouse/mice, and don't forget the words that have the same form for both singular and plural: moose, sheep, deer, pants, underwear, species, aircraft, police, and so on.

Rule of thumb: When in doubt, look it up.

### Plurals of common nouns.

When common nouns are plural, referring to two or more places or things, do not capitalize them.

Examples:

Our offices are located on Magnolia Street, which is between Dogwood and Crape Myrtle streets. (Not "Streets.")

Bowdoin and Colby colleges are in Maine. (Not "Colleges.")

**Plurals of proper nouns.**

Names of persons and other capitalized nouns normally form the plural by adding "s" or *-es*.

Examples:

Larry, Curly, Moe turn into Larrys, Curlys, and Moes

the Sloanes family turns into the Sloaneses

the Ramirez family turns into the Ramirezes

the DiCarlo family turns into the DiCarlos

Hindu turns into Hindus

An apostrophe is never used to form the plural of a family name: "The Smiths live here" (not the "Smith's"). The Smiths' would be the possessive: The Smiths' house, meaning, The Smith family's house. Similarly, the Sloaneses' home, the Ramirezes' home, etc.

**Compound nouns.**

A dictionary will give the plural form of most compounds that are tricky (attorneys general, mothers-in-law, aides-de-camp, coups de foudre, letters to the editor, turns of phrase, passers by (or passersby), calls-to-action, courts-martial, etc.).

**Plural form of italicized words.**

If italicized terms—names of newspapers, titles of books, and the like—are used in the plural, the "s" is normally set in the regular, nonitalicized version of the font. A title already in plural form, however, may be left unchanged. In case of doubt, avoid the plural by rephrasing. The plural endings of italicized foreign words should also be set in italics.

**Plural form for words and phrases in quotation marks.**

This can be difficult. Most of the time it is best to consider rephrasing your sentence to avoid doing so: never add an "s" outside quotation marks to form a plural. However, forming a plural inside quotation marks can be done.

Example: There was Georgie, under Lucia's very nose, interlarding his conversation with far more "Elizabeths" than was in the least necessary to show that he was talking to her, and she volleyed "Georgies" at him in return.

**More tricky plurals.**

Words and hyphenated phrases that are not nouns but are used as nouns usually form the plural by adding "s" or *-es*. When in doubt, consult a recent edition of an unabridged dictionary, which will indicate the preferred forms for most nouns, including the examples below:

thank-yous ("thank yous" would also be okay; never thank you's)

maybes

ifs, ands, or buts; ins and outs

dos and don'ts (*not* do's and don'ts, which I saw in a biography of Judy Garland the other day)

yeses and nos (or "noes")

**Plurals for letters, abbreviations, and numerals.**

Capital letters used as words, numerals used as nouns, and abbreviations usually form the plural by adding "s." To make them easier to read, single letters form the plural with an apostrophe + "s." Examples:

p's and q's, A's and B's, x's and o's

the three R's

the 1990s

IRAs, UPCs, CPAs, MRIs

BAs, MBAs, JDs, PhDs (for more on titles, see the "Titles and honorifics" section)

vols.

eds.

But:

p. (page), pp. (pages)

n. (note), nn. (notes)

MS (manuscript), MSS (manuscripts)

Note: Some style manuals (*Chicago*) call for the apostrophe + "s" only for lowercase single letters, so you will see "As" and "Bs" from time to time, and...it's correct, but there is quite a bit to be said for consistency: I suggest that you consider apostrophe + "s" for both lower- *and* uppercase single letters.

## The Possessive.

### Forming Possessives of Nouns

To decide if you need to create a possessive, turn the phrase around and make it an "of the..." phrase.

Examples:

the child's hamster = the hamster of the (belonging to) child

a year's worth of problems = problems of a year

It is not always necessary to specify what is being possessed; the reader can be allowed to infer what it is.

Example: From there he went down past the fishmonger's, crossed the road, and doubled back again up Puffin's side of the street, which was not so vividly illuminated, though he took the precaution of making himself little with bent knees, and of limping.

In this example, the reader knows that the author is referring to the fishmonger's "shop" or "place of business."

**Forming the possessive of singular nouns.**

Examples: woman's, weather's, church's, the business's financials, the horse's bridle, my fax's ink

However, it is still considered correct to use an apostrophe only after the names of biblical or historical figures that end in "s": Jesus' trial, Moses' laws, Achilles' heel.

And, if the noun is a) singular, b) ends with an "s" or a "z" sound, and c) the next word starts with an "s," then use the apostrophe by itself to form the possessive.

Examples: the service' sign, the cheese' sharpness, politeness' sake

**Forming the possessive of plural nouns.**

When creating the possessive of a plural noun, add only the apostrophe:

Example: The horses' saddles, the Norrises' home

**To recap:**

Cindy Norris (singular noun)

Cindy Norris's black truck (singular possessive)

The Norrises are coming tomorrow (plural noun)

The Norrises' black truck (plural possessive)

**Correctly showing ownership.**

To show common ownership, use an apostrophe (with an "s" when appropriate) after the last thing/person listed.

Example: Ben and Jerry's New York Super Chunk Fudge is my favorite, I'm sorry to say.

The previous example showed that both Ben and Jerry "own" New York Super Chunk Fudge.

If, however, you want to illustrate individual ownership, you must use a possessive pronoun or an apostrophe after each person/thing (and maybe an "s") referred to.

Examples:

James's and Mary's Porsche 911s are almost identical.

His and Mary's Porsche 911s are almost identical.

**Tricky possessives.**

Don't forget: there's a big, big, big difference between a possessive and a contraction.

*Its*, not *it's*, is the possessive form of "it": it's = *it is*.

*Whose*, not *who's*, is the possessive form of "who"; who's = *who is*.

There is no possessive of the word *that*. There is an apostrophe + "s" contraction of *that*—*that's*, which means *that is*—but there is no possessive. The possessive of *that* is *whose*. This sentence is incorrect:

She also founded the Houston Tweet Drive—an annual social media-driven event that's success has donated more than 1,000 toys to local charities.

"People" is the plural of *person*. The possessive of *people* is *people's*: The people's will was carried out.

However, "people" could also be used to refer to "peoples," as in "The indigenous peoples of the North." The possessive of *peoples* in that case would be *peoples'*. (It would be difficult to use peoples' without some prior reference to "peoples.")

**Common mistakes.**

Be careful when you have a word that ends in an "s." Here are two very easy mistakes to make with words that end in "s."

If you could substitute the word *of* in a sentence, you need an apostrophe after the word.

Correct: I have seven years of experience.

Correct: I have seven years' experience.

Incorrect: I have seven years experience.

Worse: I have seven year's experience.

This is a very common mistake, particularly when writing biographical information.

Here's a variation of the "years of experience" sentence. It is incorrect because it needs an apostrophe with *years:*

This certification is awarded to hospitality executives upon the completion of 20 days of Lausanne Executive Education with LHC within 3 years time.

## The Descriptive Phrase Rule.

Sometimes you'll have a situation when a phrase with a word that ends in an "s" looks like it should be possessive, but isn't.

Example: She is also a member of the XYZ Bar Association and active with its Young Lawyers' Division.

If you can substitute *by* or *for* in the longer version of a phrase, which, in this case, would be "a division for young lawyers," then what you have is not a possessive but a descriptive phrase—no apostrophe.

## Question marks.

A question mark is used at the end of a sentence that contains a query or at the end of a query that makes up part of a sentence.

Examples:

Clearly she had been to inspect it, or how could she have got the keys?

Would you know how to do it? was the question I was asking.

A question mark can be used to indicate uncertainty.

Example: Edward Teach (c. 1680?—22 November 1718)

(For more about using question marks in dialog, please see the "Quotation marks" section that follows.)

## Quotation marks.

In American English, commas and periods are always placed *inside* quotation marks, whether the quotation marks are single or double. There are no exceptions—commas and periods are *always* placed inside quotation marks.

**Important note:** In British English, the rules regarding quotation marks are completely the opposite: periods and commas outside, and the order is single, double, single, not double, single, double. If you are writing for American English speakers in the American market, follow *American* rules.

This section discusses the use of quotation marks primarily in written dialog. If you are looking for information about how to quote someone else's words, please refer to the Quotations section.

Note: Watch the direction of your quotation marks. Sometimes, when using Microsoft Word, you'll have to play around with the quotation marks to make them face the right way.

### Quotation marks in conversation.

It's official: No one knows how to punctuate written dialog anymore.

Quotation marks generally come in pairs, with an important exception discussed below.

When starting a quotation at the beginning of a sentence, always capitalize the first word.

Example: "Delighted," said Georgie, though he had ordered oysters.

When quotation marks are used when quoting exactly what was said, that is called a *direct* quote.

Example: Nobody seemed to believe Elizabeth's assertion that there was "nothing in it."

In conversation, when quoting something that was said at another time (even if you said it), use single quotes *inside* the larger structure of the double quotes. The structure is "This-and-that 'then thus-and-so' and that's how you do it."

Examples:

"She wanted you very much—she said 'particularly Lucia'—to go to lunch or dine with her on Sunday. Peppino, too, of course."

"Hardly a note," said Georgie; "there is nobody to play with. Piggy wanted to do some duets, but I said 'No, thanks.'"

In the rare situation when someone is speaking and is quoting someone else who was quoting someone else, the structure is: Double Quote (always) + Single Quote + Double Quote + Single Quote + (always) Double Quote. Double quotation marks *always* go outside either single quotation marks or single + double quotation marks.

Example: "And then I heard him say 'Gosh, Liz told me that she "hated" okra!'"

If you see writing that does not follow this structure, it's likely British English.

Some authors separate the double/single, single/double quotes with a space, and that's okay, as long as you do it consistently.

**Quotation marks in a lengthy conversation.**

When a character speaks for long enough to necessitate a new paragraph, do not use end quotes ( " ) at the conclusion of the paragraph; instead, start the new paragraph with quotation marks and continue to where he or she stops speaking and *then* use end quotes. This is the exception to the "quotation marks come in pairs" rule.

Here is the *Watership Down* storytelling quote I used earlier. See those beginning quotes? See that there are no end quotes after the word "rain"? See how the parentheses interrupt? So you would expect that if the speaker keeps speaking (and, indeed, that is what happens), the line following the end parenthesis to begin with double quotes, like so:

> "The next day in the afternoon, it began to rain.
> ("Those scrapes we dug in the bank," whispered Buckthorn to Dandelion.)
>
> "Everyone was underground, just chewing pellets or sleeping...."

**Punctuation marks with quotation marks.**

When a direct quote is followed by "he said" or "she remarked" or some other method of attribution and/or conversational description, like "Mary shrieked loudly," the quote is followed by the attribution and a period if the sentence is finished, or a comma if it continues.

Example: "I hardly know whether there's a lemon left," he grumbled.

Example: "Thank God I live on a hill," exclaimed Major Benjy, thinking, as usual, of himself.

When a direct quote is interrupted in the middle of a sentence, don't capitalize the beginning of the second part of the sentence.

Example: "But I got that bottle in only the day before yesterday," he shouted, "and there's hardly a drink left in it."

When a person's dialog is modified, for example, "...he said calmly," or "...she announced firmly," don't put a comma between the "said" or "announced" and the way the words were said or announced. If the word or words directly relate to the way the dialog was spoken, screamed, sung, or yelled, then there is no comma between it/them. However, if you described how the words were said in a way that doesn't answer the question of how the dialog was delivered, then there is a comma between "said" and the word.

Consider these examples:

“Clever of her,” said Lucia appreciatively.

“No!” said Georgie with a livelier inflection.

“And what’s the matter exactly, chérie?” asked Elizabeth, oozing with the tenderest curiosity.

“I’ll go,” she said, smiling.

When describing dialog—not actually quoting dialog—in the middle of a sentence, the rule of thumb is to include any exclamation points or question marks, but to use a comma instead of a period.

Examples:

And not a word about expectations!...Lucia’s dear Daisy crumpled up the absurd note and said, “Rubbish,” so loud that Georgie Pillson in the next garden thought he was being addressed.

“No, three hundred Siriami,” said Elizabeth, and Diva heard. Simultaneously, Diva’s young lady asked, “Is it Siriami?” and Elizabeth heard.

**Exclamation points and question marks can go inside or outside quotation marks.**

The placement of a question mark or exclamation point in dialog depends on the context.

Example: “Hullo, Hopkins, are you ready?” said Irene.

In this example, Irene’s comment is phrased as a question. Instead of “said,” she could have “asked.” So, the question mark goes *inside* the quotation marks.

Example: And then what did the gallant Lucia’s final words mean, when she said “Just wait till we come back”?

In this example, Lucia did not say "Just wait till we come back?" What she said was "Just wait till come back." Other people are now speculating (hence, the question mark) about exactly what Lucia meant when she said what she said. So, the question mark goes *outside* the quotation marks. The exact same rule applies to quotation marks and exclamation points.

Take a look at this sentence:

Are any Boar's Head products made with "pink slime?"

Clearly, the question mark should have been placed *outside* the quotation mark: Are any Boar's Head products made with "pink slime"?

Here is another good example. This sentence, from *The Hunt for Red October*, is incorrect (sorry, Mr. Clancy!):

"Excuse me, what is this 'kludge?'"

In the previous example, the speaker is questioning the definition of a word, so the single quote should have been placed *inside* the question mark, like so: "Excuse me, what is this 'kludge'?"

If this were not dialog, the sentence would look like this:

Excuse me, what is this "kludge"?

**No quotation marks for paraphrasing.**

Quotation marks are not used when someone is reporting the gist of a conversation (an *indirect* quote) and making no representation that the quote is exactly what that person said.

Example: He said something about visiting sometime, but I never imagined he would.

**Be careful when writing dialog.**

No matter how many speakers are conversing at the same time, each time the speaker changes a new paragraph is created, even if a speaker says one word. Note: Make sure your speakers are identified unambiguously. If two men are talking and you write “he said” this and “he said” that—after that happens a time or two you run the risk of confusing your readers.

Example:

“Yes?” said Daisy and Georgie simultaneously.

“So you’ve been calculating too?” said Mr. Quantock. “Might have a sweepstake for the one who gets nearest. I say three thousand a year.”

“Not so much,” said Georgie and Daisy again simultaneously.

“All right. But that’s no reason why I shouldn’t have a lump of sugar in my tea.”

“Dear me, no,” said Daisy genially. “But how do you make it up to three thousand?”

“By addition,” said this annoying man. “There’ll be every penny of that. I was at the lending library after lunch, and those who could add made it all that.”

Because Georgie and Daisy are being considered as a unit, by process of elimination we understand that the “annoying man” referred to in this passage was Mr. Quantock and not “Georgie.” It’s best to be specific.

**Quotation marks are also used when speaking of a word as a word.**

Examples:

This simple word “No” connoted a great deal in the Riseholme vernacular.

But never yet had “baffled” sullied her wells of pure undefiled English.

Note: nowadays, it is also acceptable to use italics in this situation. Before the age of the word processor, italics were difficult to create. However, consider the fact that italics are also used for emphasis. In my opinion, it often makes things easier for your readers if you make it a habit to put quotation marks around the use of a word as a "word" and employ italics for emphasis, though, admittedly, italics look cleaner, especially if you are using words in a list: too many quotation marks can look confusing.

The main thing is to be consistent throughout your work.

**Quotation marks can be used to indicate a trendy, perhaps slangy expression.**

If the person speaking incorporates a slangy or popular expression into his or her conversation, use single quotes around the word or expression. If the slangy expression is not involved in a conversation, use double quotes.

Example: "She was 'all over me,' to use that dreadful slang expression of Major Benjy's," continued Mapp.

Example: It was true that she, in popular parlance, was "getting on," but so, too, and at exactly the same rate, were the representatives of the United Services, and the sooner that two of the three of them "got on" permanently, the better.

Note that in the first example the trendy expression was put inside single quotes, since it was *said*. Remember the rule: Single quotes inside double quotes. In the second example, the expression is put inside double quotes because there is no conversation going on at the time the expression is introduced.

Note that both of those examples contain commas *inside* quotation marks.

**Quotation marks can indicate sarcasm or irony.**

Example: It was the Major's turn to entertain his friend, and by half past nine, on a certain squally October evening, he and Puffin were seated by the fire in his "study," while the rain volleyed at the windows and occasional puffs of stinging smoke were driven down the chimney and into the room by the gale that squealed and buffeted around the house.

That was certainly an example of when it would be better to use quotes, as opposed to italics, to convey your use of irony when writing about the Major's "study."

**Quotation marks used for thoughts.**

When quoting internal thought, you may use quotation marks or italics—italics have become more common (and look cleaner), though both are correct—but the main thing is to be consistent throughout your work: use one or the other but not both.

Example: "A little diplomacy," thought Georgie, as he trotted across to her house after breakfast with no hat, but a fur tippet round his neck.

It would be incorrect to use both quotation marks and italics for thoughts. This would be incorrect: "*A little diplomacy*," thought Georgie.

When you are writing in the first person and illustrating your own personal thought, italics are more appropriate and make your purpose—expressing personal, unspoken thoughts—crystal clear to your readers. If you need to add emphasis when using italics, change the font back to its regular, nonitalicized form.

However, you run the risk of confusing your readers if you have a character "thinking" while speaking to one or more other characters; in other words, instead of "he said" and "she said," you have a character expressing an opinion out loud, as in "he thought." That's difficult for the reader because a "thought" is generally unexpressed. A very famous author has gotten into this habit, and it's most unfortunate.

Example:

"I did it," she said.

"You're going to be punished," he thought.

"I agree," Monica chimed in.

It's only after reviewing the conversation that the reader understands the male character's "thought" was spoken out loud. When a reader has to review your writing to figure out what you meant, it's not a good thing.

**Quotation marks and titles.**

Use quotations marks for:

Titles of short or minor works
Songs
Short poems
Short stories
Essays
One-act plays
Chapters in books
Other literary works shorter than a three-act play or complete book
Titles of sections from longer works
Articles in newspapers, magazines, or websites
Episodes of television and radio series (but the series itself should be italicized)
Computer games

Generally speaking, italics are used for the titles of books, record albums, or works that contain smaller sections. Think about a pie. The title of the "pie" is italicized, and the slices—the individual pieces—are put in quotation marks.

A sentence like this is not just wrong, it's really wrong:

So, they wrote a blog article, *"Legal Separation in PA: The Great Myth"* that shot their rank for the phrase up to #1.

You would never use both quotation marks and italics when specifying an article. In this case, quotation marks alone are what's necessary. Plus, the author missed the comma after the article title. The sentence should read:

So, they wrote a blog article, "Legal Separation in PA: The Great Myth," that shot their rank for the phrase up to #1.

Note: the "style" used by newspapers is not necessarily the style that should be used by the authors of books, articles, website content, blogs, essays, term papers, etc. Newspapers never use a serial comma (sources seem to agree that this style arose in the olden days of typesetting more because of the ease of simply not including that last comma than for any other reason), and newspapers will put some things—like the series name of a television show—in quotes ("Batman," instead of *Batman*).

**Single quotation marks.**

It is acceptable, though not necessary, to use single quotes to specify a type or breed of plant or animal: 'Patty Pan' squash, 'Liz Taylor' rose, 'Tea Cup' poodle.

Except for the rule above, in American English single quotation marks are only used within double quotation marks. A sentence like this is really wrong:

The Family Law Center wanted to add a human component to the divorce process through coaching and planning, positioning itself as the firm that is 'restoring sanity and dignity to the divorce process'.

Double quotation marks are needed; plus, this author ran afoul of the quotation-marks-always-go-outside-periods-and-commas rule.

Here is the corrected sentence:

The Family Law Center wanted to add a human component to the divorce process through coaching and planning, positioning itself as the firm that is "restoring sanity and dignity to the divorce process."

## Quotations.

This section is about how to properly punctuate someone else's writing when you incorporate it into your text; if you are looking for how to use quotation marks, please refer to the "Quotation mark" section.

What we're trying to do here is anticipate the various uses of quotation marks in nonacademic fiction and nonfiction, so if you are writing a research paper, please consult your instructor and ask what specific format you need to follow. Ditto footnotes. There are so many styles of footnotes that footnotes are beyond the scope of this manual; your instructor will instruct you, so ask.

**Accuracy is *key*.**

When you quote someone else's work, you've got to be accurate. Don't rely on memory: check and double-check. The entire quote must be incorporated seamlessly into your narrative, though you can choose to quote just a word or phrase. If you do make a change to someone else's original language, you must make whatever you are changing (using brackets) completely clear to your reader. You could also paraphrase someone else's work, but even then you've got to give the author proper attribution.

There are a number of options as far as quoting goes. You have the option of giving attribution for the quote immediately following it, doing an on-page footnote, or a footnote that leads the reader to a footnote list at the end of the text. Some authors list the entities that gave permission for the use of copyrighted works at the beginning of their text, before their article or blog even starts. This is a nice way to handle attribution, because it gets the attributions out of the way of the narrative.

The primary function of quotation marks in this context is to set off and represent exact language (either spoken or written) that you are borrowing from somebody else. It is important to properly credit other people for their words.

**The quote at the beginning of a section of text.**

A brief, appropriate quotation used to introduce a certain concept and indicate a change of focus is the most common kind of quote. This is a stand-alone quote, appearing above the text. If you do it once, you should to do it for every section of the piece.

The introductory quote is generally very short—a phrase or handful of sentences. Quotation marks are optional, especially if the quote is a sentence or less in length or if the quote is set off by a different font. The quote and source should be indented or centered. A writer will often change the font, the size of the font, center the quote, or italicize the quote to distinguish it from the rest of the text. The author of the quote must be named, but the source is optional. If the source is a book, then the title of the book needs to be italicized; put quotation marks around the titles of short stories or poems.

And those are *dashes* in front of the authors' names, not hyphens.

Here are several options:

...It was one of the great livery-stableman's most masterly intuitions to have discovered that Americans want to get away from amusement even more quickly than they want to get to it.

—Edith Wharton, *The Age of Innocence*

Scatter joy.

—RALPH WALDO EMERSON

*A little thing comforts us because a little thing afflicts us.*

—PASCAL

**Quotations within the text.**

The way you'll acknowledge someone else's work within your narrative will be determined by the length of the quote. There are two types of quotes: short ones and long ones. You should introduce the quotation by using a colon.

**Short quotations.**

If a prose quotation runs four lines or fewer, put it in quotation marks and incorporate it into your text.

If you are quoting poetry or lyrics, the rules are similar. If quoting an entire line or a part of a line, put the section between quotation marks within your text. If what you quote crosses a line of the poem or lyrics itself, show the reader where all line breaks occur by using a slash; either skip a space on both sides of the slash or don't skip any, but be consistent. Include any punctuation exactly as it is in the original source.

Example:

In the Prologue to *Romeo and Juliet*, Shakespeare immediately warns his audience not to expect a happy ending by having the chorus talk about "A pair of star-crossed lovers," who spring from the "fatal loins" of "two foes."

That sounds like a research paper. Here are a couple of examples of how to incorporate a quote into a nonacademic text.

"You know, I can quote several poems," remarked Liz, looking out the window.

"No kidding," replied Stan, impressed. "Like what?"

"Well, let's see. I can quote several long passages from *Romeo and Juliet*, the first stanza of 'The Tiger,' by Robert Blake, and 'Stopping by the Woods on a Snowy Evening,' by Robert Frost." She paused. "I could probably get through 'The Journey of the Magi,' by T. S. Eliot, if I had to, though it's been a while. You want to hear one?"

"Sure."

"Which one?" Liz asked, hoping he wouldn't ask for something from *Romeo and Juliet*. Or "The Journey of the Magi," for that matter....How long had it been since she'd recited that? Years, absolute years.

"How about 'The Tiger,'" he said, grinning. "Does it have anything to do with Clemson?"

"Oh, no." She said, smiling back. "Blake lived in the 1700s—when Clemson wasn't even a twinkle in anyone's eye. Don't make this into an ACC thing!"

They laughed.

"All right," she said. "My father taught this to me-when I was really young: four, maybe. My mother says he used to get me up in front of people to recite it, like a dog doing tricks. I had no idea what it meant." She laughed without humor. "Still don't."

She silently counted to five and took a breath. "Okay, here goes: 'Tiger, tiger, burning bright/In the forests of the night/What immortal hand or eye/Could frame thy fearful symmetry?'"

Stan tapped his palm on the steering wheel by way of applause. "Nice!"

"Nah," she said, smiling. "Easy."

Here's another example:

Edith Wharton was an astute observer of the human condition. I particularly like this quote, and I don't even know what work it's from: "Her failure was a useful preliminary to success." It makes me feel brave, somehow, since I've failed a time or two.

**Long quotations.**

Long quotations—quotations of poetry or prose longer than four lines—are sometimes called block quotations because they are set off in the text.

Typically, a block quotation is indented ten spaces "in" from the left margin. If the block quotation is part of a dialog, skip one space between the beginning of the quotation and the text; if the block quotation is not part of a dialog, then skip two spaces. Block quotations are not enclosed by quotation marks. Most authors change the font and/or font size to announce the presence of someone else's words in their narrative.

**Using block quotations at the beginning of a chapter or section.**

This is a very typical use of block quotations. You'll want to indent ten spaces from the left margin, and several spaces from the right, just enough to make a difference.

Example:

> Though it was nearly a year since her husband's death, Emmeline Lucas (universally known to her friends as Lucia) still wore the deepest and most uncompromising mourning. Black certainly suited her very well, but that had nothing to do with this continued use of it, whatever anybody said.
> —E. F. Benson, *Mapp and Lucia*

Note that the author's name follows the quote, preceded by a dash (not a hyphen!); that the work the quote comes from is either on that same line or on the next line; and is either italicized (if a book) or enclosed in quotation marks (if a poem, short story, or lyrics). If you want to indent the author's name and source further from the left-hand margin (say, four lines or so), that is up to you.

You could also acknowledge both author and source within the body of your text, like so:

My absolute favorite opening passage in a book is this description of Miss Mapp, in E. F. Benson's immortal *Miss Mapp*. I bet Mr. Benson worked hard to achieve such wordy mastery. Don't you just love it?

> Miss Elizabeth Mapp might have been forty, and she had taken advantage of this opportunity by being just a year or two older. Her face was of a high vivid color and corrugated by chronic rage and curiosity; but these vivifying emotions had preserved to her an astonishing activity of mind and body, which fully accounted for the comparative adolescence which she would have been credited anywhere except in the charming little town which she had inhabited so long. Anger and the gravest suspicions about everybody had kept her young and on the boil.

The key thing, like so many other things in writing, is to be consistent throughout your work.

**Using block quotations in dialog.**

Let's try the "poetry quotation" conversation, when Liz is bragging to Stan again, with a longer quote.

"I can quote several poems," remarked Liz.

"No kidding," replied Stan, impressed. "Like what?"

"Well, I can quote several long passages from *Romeo and Juliet;* the first stanza of 'The Tiger,' by Robert Blake; T. S. Eliot's 'The Journey of the Magi'; and 'Stopping by the Woods on a Snowy Evening,' by Robert Frost. You want to hear one?"

"Sure."

"Which one?" Liz asked, hoping he wouldn't ask for something from *Romeo and Juliet.* Or "The Journey of the Magi," for that matter.

"How about something from *Romeo and Juliet,*" he said, grinning. "That would be appropriate." Seeing her raise her eyebrows, he added quickly, "Because of the 'true love' stuff, not the tragic parts."

"Okay. Do you want the opening prologue, or the Prince's last speech?"

"I don't know. You choose."

Liz wrinkled her brow and offered up a brief prayer to the gods of poetry, asking that she could get over that one part where she always tripped up. She counted to five—for drama's sake—took a deep breath, and began, picturing Zeffirelli's *Romeo and Juliet* as she spoke:

> Two households, both alike in dignity,
> In fair Verona, where we lay our scene,
> From ancient grudge break to new mutiny,
> Where civil blood makes civil hands unclean.
> From forth the fatal loins of these two foes
> A pair of star-cross'd lovers take their life;
> Whose misadventur'd piteous overthrows

Doth with their death bury their parents' strife.

"Wow!" said Stan, tapping his palm on the steering wheel to indicate clapping. "Good job!"

"Oh, there's a little more," Liz said, pleased with his response, "but that's the important bit."

**Quoting someone else's letter, note, poetry, or other writing in a "nonacademic" setting.**

When you are quoting someone else's letter, poetry, or other writing in a "nonacademic" setting (e.g., a nonresearch setting, such as a blog, article, and so on), the way the quotation will be displayed in your narrative needs to be distinguished from the body of your text, and that is generally accomplished by either indenting, changing the font, or both. For example, if you use a love letter in your text, whether it is a real love letter or a fabrication, it must be obvious to your readers that this is a separate and distinct section of the narrative.

The easy way to "set off" the written words is to downsize your font a tad, just enough so you can see the difference. Skip a space between the regular text and the quote, indent at the beginning of the quote and throughout the quote as necessary, and skip a space when you transition back between the quote and the text. When typing the signature of the person being quoted, use capital letters in the same, smaller font.

Here is an example from *Make Way for Lucia*. This is a portion of a letter written from Georgie to Lucia. We start with Lucia's picking up Georgie's letter and then reading it.

> ...She turned first to Georgie's letter.
> The most wonderful thing has happened [wrote Georgie] and you will be pleased....There's a family here with whom I've made friends: an English teacher, an Italian mother, and a little girl with a pigtail. Listen!

..............................................................................

I'm having quite a gay time, music and drives and seeing the Channel boats come in, and aren't I clever?
Your devoted,
GEORGIE

**Quoting someone else in an academic situation.**

Besides using quotation marks when quoting dialog, the most common use of quotation marks is in a more academic situation, when you quote a passage written by someone else.

The primary function of quotation marks is to set off and represent exact language (either spoken or written) that has come from somebody else. It is important to properly credit other people for their words and distinguish their words from yours.

Quotation marks are used for shorter quotes, typically those of three or four lines, which are incorporated directly into the body of your text.

Note: don't go overboard with direct quotations, even in a research paper, because your readers want to read what you have to say about the topic, not what everyone else has said.

Many writers struggle when deciding to use direct quotations versus indirect quotations. It is very important to give other authors proper credit whenever appropriate within your own writing, regardless of whether the quote is direct or indirect, so that you can't be accused of plagiarism.

It is a good idea to establish an appropriate style for this issue and be consistent in its use.

**Direct quotations.**

Use direct quotations when the source material uses language that is unique, notable, and quotable. When an author has coined a unique word or phrase, always use quotation marks around that word or phrase.

Example: As far as I know, California Licensed Land Surveyor and Certified Fraud Examiner David Woolley, in his June 2011, white paper, "MERS: The

Unreported Effects of Lost Chain of Title on Real Property Owners," coined the phrase "wild title" to describe a property whose chain of title has been broken: by fraud, by MERS, or both.

Note: When you are quoting material and there is a misspelling or other mistake in the original and you want to make sure your reader knows it's not your mistake, write "sic" and put it in brackets, like this: [sic]. "Sic" is Latin and translates into "thus," "so," or "just as that." Using [sic] tells your readers that you are transcribing the original faithfully as written, warts and all.

**Indirect Quotations.**

Use an indirect quotation (or paraphrase) when you merely need to summarize key incidents or details of the text.

In this case, it is not necessary to use quotation marks. However, indirect quotations still require proper attribution, and you will be committing plagiarism if you fail to do so.

## Semicolons.

Semicolons have a variety of uses; unlike commas, dashes, and parentheses, a semicolon does not indicate a pause or the insertion of additional information.

Use a semicolon when you link two (or more) independent clauses with no connecting words.

Examples:

Verboten; défendu; non permesso.

I am going home; I intend to stay there.

They couldn't make it to the summit and back before dark; they decided to camp for the night.

This use is incorrect:

"Shotgun" approaches, where one includes every cause of action they can possible think of, is not strategic; and can often be harmful.

That semicolon should not be there because "and can often be harmful" is not a complete sentence. There are also *three* other mistakes in this sentence; did you catch them?

Answer: The subject, "approaches," is plural, which means "is" is incorrect; "one" is singular, so you cannot use "they"; and "possible" should be "possibly." Geesh!

You also use a semicolon when you join two independent clauses together with one of the following conjunctive adverbs: *after all, also, as a result, besides, consequently, finally, for example, furthermore, however, in addition, in fact, in other words, incidentally, indeed, instead, likewise, nevertheless, next, nonetheless, on the contrary, on the other hand, otherwise, meanwhile, moreover, still, then, thus.*

main clause + SEMICOLON + conjunctive adverb + comma + main clause

Examples:

I am going home; moreover, I intend to stay there.

They couldn't make it to the summit and back before dark; therefore, they decided to camp for the night.

A semicolon will often be used when the second clause reveals a striking contrast to the first clause, or when the main clause contains at least one comma.

Use a semicolon to join elements in a list when at least one item includes a comma or internal punctuation.

Example:

She had seen no pictures lately, except Bobbie (or was it Bertie?) Alton's; she had heard no music; she had not touched the piano herself for weeks; she had read no books, and at the most had skimmed the reviews of such as had lately appeared in order to be up to date and be able to reproduce a short but striking criticism or two if the talk became literary.

So, having read that, what's wrong with this sentence?

Mr. Bird is on the panel of mediators of the United States District Court, Southern District of New York, and the rosters of mediators of the American Arbitration Association, the Commercial Division of the Supreme Court of the State of New York, County of New York, and the Coop and Condo Panel of the NYCBA.

What's wrong is that one of the items in this list—the Commercial Division of the Supreme Court of the State of New York, County of New York—has internal punctuation, triggering the need for, you guessed it, semicolons.

Skip one space after a semicolon.

If you need to use semicolons in a list, place them throughout; in other words, you must use one in front of the last item as well.

Example: Do not use a colon after verbs or prepositional phrases such as *includes; including; including, but not limited to; consists of; such as;* and *for example.*

The one item in this list that triggered the use of semicolons was the phrase *including, but not limited to;* without that phrase, commas would have been used throughout.

(There is also additional information about semicolons in the Comma section.)

## Using a slash.

When you want to convey equal parts of something, use a slash (/) between co-equal nouns, as opposed to a hyphen.

Examples: OB/GYN, 24/7, 9/11, the Huntoon/Coursen team, work/life balance

The thought behind this rule is that a hyphen could be misinterpreted to indicate a single hyphenated name, like Huntoon-Coursen, but the slash makes it clear that each side of the slash constitutes a distinct entity.

A slash can also indicate *per* (meaning, for each), as in $10/hour.

A slash is also used to separate lines of poetry when they are quoted within the text, and not as a block quotation.

Some style manuals suggest skipping a space, then using the slash, and skipping another space, but...what's the point of all those spaces?

## That vs. Who, Who vs. Whom, That vs. Which

### That vs. Who.

The relative pronouns *who* and *whom* (the latter no longer as common in American English) are used for people, *which* is used for things, and *that* is used for both. Most of the time, writers decide to use *that* to refer to a company or an organization (which is always an *it* and could never be a *who*), and use *who*, as opposed to *that*, to refer to a person or to a group of people; for example, The boy who..., The student who..., The teachers who.... Use "that" for collective nouns: The teachers' union that..., The football team that....

In other words, if you could substitute *he, she, them,* or *they* for the noun, use *who* and not *that*. If, on the other hand, you could very easily substitute *it* for the noun, as in the case of most collective nouns, *that* is correct: the team that wins, the staff that strikes, the group that meets, and so on.

Look at this sentence:

*The Swarm* is an ongoing series about a young woman that must defy the odds, both natural and supernatural, in her quest to become a queen among men.

No! The "young woman who..." ("A queen among men"? Geesh!)

Here's another, similar, sentence:

She earned two "Book Awards," a distinction given to the student that achieved the highest grade in a particular class.

No! The "student who..."

Consider this sentence:

This is a great tool for any agency who needs to provide their clients relevant content in a timely fashion.

Why would an "agency" be considered a "who"? And "agency" is singular, so how can an agency be "their"? Plus, "every" is more upbeat, more inclusive than "any."

Corrected, the sentence reads:

This is a great tool for every agency that needs to provide its clients relevant content in a timely fashion.

**Important point.** There is no possessive of "that." *Whose* is the possessive of both *who* and *that*: The team whose jerseys were blue..., The girl whose hair was blond...

**Who vs. whom.**

In American English, *whom* is not used very often. *Whom* is more formal than *who* and is very often omitted when speaking:

Grammatically correct: The man to whom you have just spoken is my minister.

Conversational use:

The man you have just spoken to is my minister.

The man you just spoke to is my minister.

The man who you have just spoken to is my minister.

However, “whom” may not be omitted if preceded by a preposition because the pronoun functions as the object of the preposition:

The people for whom I worked have moved across town.

That sounds very stiff. Here’s a more conversational version:

The people I worked for have moved across town.

**Easy (easy-ish) way to remember:** If you can flip a sentence around and use *he* in the sentence, use *who*; if you can use *him* in the sentence, use *whom.* Try it. It works!

Example:

You just spoke to that man.

You spoke to *him.*

He is my minister.

The man to whom you have just spoken is my minister.

We’re in deep weeds here. You can also say:

You just spoke to my minister.

**That vs. Which.**

*That* is used to restrict meaning of a sentence; in other words, the information following *that* is essential to the meaning of the sentence.

Examples:

The Padre, with his new umbrella, ran down the steps that led to the road below in order to hook it in if it approached within umbrella distance.

Which steps were they? The ones that led to the road.

During her deposition testimony in *In re Wilson*, Dory Goebel described the procedures that she followed to create robo-signed affidavits. (In this use, "re" is pronounced "ray." You pre-law people ought to learn that now.)

Which procedures were followed? The ones to create affidavits.

The information that follows *which*, on the other hand, gives you more information (an explanation, a description, an elaboration) about the subject and, therefore, is nonrestrictive.

Example: The term "robo-signing," which describes the practice of signing hundreds of documents each day without the legally required "personal knowledge" of what each document contained, was coined during the foreclosure crisis.

Unless it follows a preposition (*in which, for which, on which,* etc.), a comma typically precedes *which;* a comma never precedes *that.*

Here's an exception: I must decide which math course to take. (which *one*)

Similarly: I must decide which math courses to take. (which *ones*)

There are two cases when *that* is more appropriate than *which*:

After the pronouns *all, any*(thing), *every*(thing), *few, little, many, much, no*(thing), *none,* and *some*(thing)

Example: All the cows that were branded in June were slaughtered in November.

And after a noun modified by a superlative adjective like *best, biggest, greatest, largest, smallest, worst*, and so on.

Examples:

This is the best editing book that I have ever read!

That was the worst date that I ever went on!

In informal, conversational American English, *that* in the previous sentences could be omitted:

This is the best editing book I have ever read!

That was the worst date I ever went on!

## Titles and honorifics.

Civil, military, religious, and professional titles are capitalized when they immediately precede a personal name and are thus used as part of the name (typically replacing the title holder's first name).

Examples: Professor Smithers, Reverend Peterson

However, if the title follows the person's name, it is not capitalized. This is difficult to do, I know. Take heart in that all proper nouns are still capitalized, as are honorifics.

When writing dialog, capitalize the title if the person is being addressed directly.

Example: "I hope you'll give me a shot, Coach."

If a title is used as part of a descriptive phrase, it is not capitalized.

Examples: former president Carter, the then prime minister Margaret Thatcher.

Note: this is not settled style. Some style manuals add a hyphen between "then" and "prime minister" to read "the then-prime minister." Plus, Microsoft Word is trying to capitalize prime minister even now....

Examples:

- the president; Barack Obama, former president of the United States; President Obama; the presidency; presidential
- the vice president; Joe Biden, vice president of the United States; Vice President Biden; vice-presidential seal

- the former secretary of state; Hillary Clinton, secretary of state; former Secretary of State Clinton or former Secretary Clinton

- the senator; the former senator from Rhode Island; former Rhode Island Senator Lincoln Chafee; Governor Chafee; Governor Chafee, Independent from Rhode Island (or I-RD)

In general, when a title—whether academic, civil, military, or religious—is used in conjunction with a person's name, the title is capitalized. Otherwise, it's not.

Some style manuals find it completely correct to drop a title or other honorific after it is used once and, following that first reference, refer to the person using his or her last name only. If you are comfortable with that practice, that's fine; consider, however, the propriety of referring to your pastor, a doctor, or an elderly person by his or her last name.

Similarly, some style manuals do not suggest using honorifics at all, so "Mrs. Jones" and "Rev. Smith" become "Jones" and "Smith." Plenty of people find that downright rude. This is one "rule" that you needn't be afraid to break. We suggest using appropriate titles and honorifics each and every time a person's name is used.

## Academic degrees.

The listing of academic degrees has not been standardized. There is disagreement about every aspect of the way to present academic information, including whether or not an academic degree is abbreviated with periods. Some style manuals forgo the periods, as in BA, MA, MS, PhD, MD, JD; however, the Yale Divinity School uses periods when listing the degrees of its faculty, as does the Harvard Law School. The main thing, since this is an unsettled style issue, is to be consistent within your text.

Likewise, the amount of information included with degrees (year granted; area(s) of specialization; location of the university (e.g., University of California-Los Angeles), and, if the location is displayed, the *way* it is displayed (e.g., University of California-Los Angeles versus University of California, Los Angeles versus University of California in Los Angeles), etc.) varies from institution to institution, as does the order in which the information is listed. One suggestion—if this is an issue for you—might be to visit the website of the college/university where you received your highest degree and copy the style used for the faculty of that school throughout your own work.

By the way, the "Princeton [University] Editorial Style Guide" likes the hyphenated location (e.g., University of California-Los Angeles). Since Princeton is one of the few universities that publishes a style guide, its opinion on this issue is worth having.

The following is a good example of why a hyphen, not a comma, is helpful in this situation:

Sam holds a BA in Economics from the University of California, Berkeley and an MBA from the University of Southern California Marshall School of Business.

Sam has two degrees: a BA and an MBA, but the comma in this sentence does not separate them; instead, it divides the BA degree into two pieces. This would be much more clear to readers:

Sam holds a BA in Economics from the University of California-Berkeley and an MBA from the University of Southern California Marshall School of Business.

Princeton states that its preferred use is to spell out the degree (e.g., Bachelor of Arts or bachelor's degree). Be sure to include the apostrophe: it's master's, not masters. If abbreviations are used, the abbreviations should include periods, so Doctor of Philosophy would be abbreviated Ph.D. In addition, according to Princeton the word "degree" should not accompany a degree abbreviation, so these two sentences would be incorrect:

A graduate of the University of Notre Dame, he received his B.B.A. degree in 1976, and was also awarded an Illinois CPA Certificate in 1976. Phil received his M.B.A. degree from Kellogg Graduate School of Management in 1977.

A bigger sin, however, of using or not using periods to represent a degree abbreviation is to be inconsistent, and use periods in one degree and no periods in another, like this:

Henry holds a B.Sc. degree in Business from the University of Utah and a MBA in Telecom Management from Golden Gate University.

There's another mistake in the previous sentence as well. Do you see it? (Hint: it's a problem with "MBA.")

Give up? It has to be *an* MBA.

Here's why it's important to do your research, especially in a biographical situation. This banker's biography on his employer's website says he got this degree:

Masters of Science, Mechanical Engineering Georgia Institute of Technology, Atlanta, GA

There is no such thing as a "Masters of Science, Mechanical Engineering" degree from Georgia Tech. There is, however, a "Master of Science in Mechanical Engineering" degree. Tech doesn't just hand out master's degrees to any Tom, Dick, or Jane, so it's a shame not to be accurate if you've worked hard enough to have one.

**Very important note.** There is a tacit understanding that when someone says that he or she "attended" a certain school or "studied" a certain subject, that person did not graduate. So when you see a sentence like this one:

Brad attended the University of Kentucky, where he studied Political Science and Public Policy.

it invariably means that no degree was conferred. Do not equivocate. When you get a degree, you *graduate* from the school, you *receive* a certain degree from a certain school, you *hold* a doctorate in [specialty here], you *attain* a specific professional designation. Note: I don't especially like *holds*, and would discourage its use. *Received* is much better.

## "Reverend" and "Honorable."

The abbreviations Rev. and Hon. are traditionally used before a full name when "the" does not precede the title. With "the," such titles should be spelled out. (The operative word here is "should," since a cursory examination of church programs from a variety of denominations finds that this rule is not always followed.)

## God.

Some writers always capitalize the pronouns *He*, *His,* and *Him* when referring to God. Some don't. Be consistent.

## "Junior," "Senior," "III," etc.

When writing someone's name with a designation such as "Junior," there is no comma between the name and the designation.

Example: Peter Warren Miller Jr. was the person we came to see.

However, when writing a name in a formal setting, such as when an envelope is addressed, do include a comma between the name and the title of the person, if the title follows the name.

## Family members.

In general, when referring to your mother, father, or other immediate family member directly (e.g., Mother and I), it is entirely appropriate to capitalize "Mother" or "Grandmother," or whatever name you used to refer to that person. However, when referring to family members indirectly, as in "...my cousin Darlene..." or "Then my father and I...," do not capitalize their name or family "title." When using a combination of family title and first or last names for grandparents, aunts, and uncles, it is traditional to capitalize the title and that person's name: Great-grandmother Huntoon, Uncle Beau, Aunt Dede (but "cousin" Anne and "godmother" Liz).

Always capitalize any nicknames you used for your parents, grandparents, siblings, and so on.

Some people capitalize "Mother," "Father," "Mom," and "Dad," and some people don't. It's up to you if you do or not, but be consistent throughout your work.

Don't forget the need for ironclad clarity within your text: if you have several people who share the same name, remind your readers who is who from time to time. Your husband Richard could become "Rich" to distinguish him from Richard, your son, and Richard, your attorney should become "Richard, my attorney," periodically. People inhabiting your narrative who share the same name happens frequently in memoir and autobiography, and—not surprisingly—less frequently in fiction.

## URLs.

In text, you do not need to bother with "http//"; the "www." has also become optional, so EditNATION.com is fine.

Do not italicize or bold a website address, simply continue in the established font. If capitalizing words within the website's name will aid in comprehension, do it.

Example:

For more information, please visit my new website, EditNATION.com.

EditNATION.com is so much easier to read than editnation.com.

Note: As people have become more familiar with the internet, it is increasingly common to see websites referred to without the "www" in front of their names, just as long as the .com, .org, or .edu (or whatever extension) is included.

Example: My website, AmericanPostcardArt.com, has been featured in *Southern Living* magazine five times, *Entrepreneur* twice, and *Town & Country* once.

When referring to an exact location on the internet, it is best to copy and paste the entire link, for accuracy's sake.

Example: You will find our Florida material at:

http://www.americanpostcardart.com/Merchant2/merchant.mv?Screen=CTGY&Store_Code=102&Category_Code=FL

Care is needed when identifying URLs in text, simply because an errant hyphen or misspelling will send your readers into the ozone.

Important note: Many magazines and newspapers use computer programs that automatically break up long words as necessary at the end of a line and insert a hyphen as the word flows to the next line. This is really bad news for internet business owners. For example, "FirstPerson-Publication.com" is not the same place as "FirstPersonPublications.com," so the smart entrepreneur will bring up—tactfully, of course—the necessity of accurately spelling his (or her!) website as often as is necessary to a newspaper or magazine reporter. Don't be shy! What good is a nice feature article if the newspaper or magazine misspells your website's name?

## Part 3: Common punctuation and grammatical pitfalls.

Though there are many set-in-stone rules about punctuation and grammar, here are two things you can do to maintain professionalism in your writing.

### 1) Be consistent.

Blogs and content need to be consistent. You can't use "non-fiction," for example, on one page and "nonfiction" on another.

Consistency is king when creating a body of work.

### 2) When in doubt, look it up.

Don't trust your memory—look up *everything*. Is it Allen, Allan, Alan, or Allyn? Is it Cathy or Kathy or Cathie or Kathie? Katie, Katy, or Katey? Charlestown or Charleston? *And* or ampersand? Yes, it's true that looking up names, dates, locations, and so on will drive you just about nuts, but it's got to be done.

Use an online dictionary to check and double-check if words have made the jump to being used as a single word. This commonly happens when the word created by the combination of the two words has a completely different, unique meaning. Take the word "dark room," meaning the place where a photographer develops photographs. One word or two? I'd say one, because a "darkroom," a place for developing photographs, is different from a room with little light, a "dark room."

You may want to come up with a list of special words you commonly use in your own writing, so you don't have to keep looking things up.

**3) Use strong, vivid words.**

Reduce your reliance on "it" and "some"; "it" and "some" are vague and imprecise. I always do a search prior to printing or publishing, just to make sure (damn sure) that each use of those wishy-washy words is absolutely necessary.

**There are three unforgivable mistakes a writer can make. Well, *four* "unforgivable" mistakes.**

- Using it's for its.
- Not proofing your work and letting sloppy errors slide. There are no "little" mistakes.
- Not having noun-verb agreement.
- Not having your pronoun-antecedents agree.

Now you know!

# Chapter 2. Words.

**Part 1: Commonly Misspelled/Misused Words**

**Part 2: Homonym list**

**Part 3: Foreign words and phrases that everyone should know**

**Take your time...get it right.**

The nice thing about writing, as opposed to speaking, is the opportunity to carefully consider and then select the precise word, the best word, to use in each instance, to allow yourself to pick and choose from the gamut of words in English (and perhaps other languages as well) until you've arrived at the word that expresses exactly what you are trying to convey to your reader. No clichés for you! You weigh your options, you go back and forth between the candidates, you take one, then another out for a test drive, and then... you choose.

Look at your words. Look at them closely. Is the word you've used the best word? Is that phrase the best phrase? Can you do better? Is "gamut" the best word, a better word than "spectrum"? When referring to words, is *gamut*, which describes a range of musical notes, a better word than *spectrum*, which describes the separation of white light into colored light? Get out your dictionary and thesaurus and see what other words could be used. Finding and then using *le mot juste* is a real joy.

## Part 1: Commonly Misspelled/Misused Words.

Words are so fun! "Word people" will discuss words like some people can argue about the merits of ACC versus SEC basketball or the joys of brownies versus cake. The following is a very incomplete list of words that are commonly misused, misunderstood, or are in a state of flux. Though language evolves and changes, there are still immutable truths and mistakes: the trick is to distinguish between using a word correctly, incorrectly, or deciding whether your word has fallen into the gray area in between (or in-between, or even...inbetween).

This section divided into two parts: a list of commonly confused/misspelled words, which can trip up the most careful writer, and a list of homonyms, which are words that sound the same but have different meanings. The homonym list is made up of words that are not (as) likely to be misused. Since all these words are all real words, they will not trigger the spell-check function of your word processor, and so are worth a review.

**A part vs. apart.** That one little space makes all the difference. Be careful. *Apart* means separate; *a part* means connected, in a group.

**A while vs. awhile**. *Awhile* is an adverb. It modifies a verb and means "for a brief period of time." Uses such as "for awhile" or "in awhile" are incorrect. *While* is a noun. Examples:

He played with my dog awhile, and then left the yard.

He played with my dog for a while, and he then left.

He played with my dog for a little while, and then left.

Do not use "while" as a substitute for *whereas* or *though.*

**Abrade vs. upbraid**. To *abrade* means to scrap off (abrasive, abrasion) and to *upbraid* means to berate, scold, speak sharply, verbally abuse someone.

**Abstruse vs. obtuse.** *Abstruse* means incomprehensible, difficult to understand, while *obtuse* means slow to comprehend, dull, blunt (in the sense of not sharp).

## Chapter 2. Words.

**Accept vs. except**. *Accept* means to take in, to receive, while *except* means to exclude.

**Access vs. assess.** Since I just, this very second, made this mistake, I thought I'd include these two words. *Access* means to gain entry, while *assess* means to evaluate. I feel like I just dodged a big, fat bullet.

**Adapt, adept, adopt**. *Adapt* means to adjust to one's surroundings; to be *adept* at something means to display expertise, while *adopt* means to accept something new: Her adept adoption of the adaptation was brilliant.

**Adverse vs. averse**. *Averse* means opposed to, reluctant; *adverse* means difficult, unfavorable, or inclement (in the sense of weather).

**Adviser vs. advisor.** The *-or* version sounds a little more important, perhaps, but the "Princeton Editorial Style Guide" likes *adviser.* I wonder if the popularity of the *-or* spelling has something to do with the acceptance of the word *advisory*. Interesting.

**Affect vs. effect**. *Affect* means to influence (to be affected by), so affected can mean influenced but it can also mean stilted and unnatural, in the sense of "Her behavior was childish and affected." *Effect* means to bring about, to cause (the effect of).

**Afflict vs. inflict.** To be *afflicted* means to be mentally or physically distressed by something (cancer, burdens); to *inflict* something (high taxes, onerous fees) means to punish or impose a burden on something/someone weaker. Both of these words are intransitive verbs. You are *afflicted with* or *by* something (always unpleasant); something (always unpleasant) is *inflicted on* you.

**Afterwards vs. afterward vs. afterword**. Right now, *afterwards* is wrong in American English. It's *afterward*, though, like "toward" and "backward," a case can be made for the "s." The reason the "s" is sneaking into speech, if not writing, is that it's easier to say a word ending in an "s," as opposed to a hard "d." Try it.

Afterwards, we adjourned to the bar.

Afterward, we adjourned to the bar.

An *afterword* is the concluding section of a book.

**Air, e're, ere, heir**. *Air* is what we breathe, *e're* means ever, and *ere* means before (ere worlds began). An *heir* is someone who inherits something from someone. Air, e're, ere, and heir are pronounced "air." Don't confuse any of these words with *err*, which means to make a mistake. Err is pronounced "er" (like you are clearing your throat), unless you are quoting "To err is human...," and then it is pronounced "air." According to *The New York Times*, using "air" as a verb (they aired the trial live) is jargon and should be avoided.

**Allot vs. a lot**. There is no such word as "alot," believe it or not. *A lot* means many, and *allot* means to set aside or divide.

**Allusion vs. illusion**. An *illusion* is something that deceives, gives a false sense of reality; an *allusion* (to allude to) is a casual reference to something else. To *elude* is to deliberately avoid.

**Altar vs. alter**. To *alter* (verb) means to change, while an *altar* (noun) is a covered table used in a church or other religious setting.

**Among vs. amongst**. There is no difference, really, though *amongst* sounds more British and old-fashioned, so perhaps you'll use amongst if writing historical fiction, but the more common word to use in the States is *among*.

**Amused vs. bemused.** To be *amused* about something is to find something funny, though not uproariously so. To be *bemused* means to be confused, lost in thought.

**Anecdote vs. antidote.** An *anecdote* is a brief account of a personal story, often amusing, while an *antidote* is a remedy or prevention against something unpleasant. *Anecdotal* refers to a finding not made scientifically: Our anecdotal findings prove that dog owners are happier than cat owners.

**Any vs. every.** If you are trying to sell someone something, most of the time you will want to say that "everyone will love this" or "everyone can use this," rather than "anyone will love this" or "anyone can use this."

## Chapter 2. Words.

Take a look at these two sentences:

I want to be the most effective, valued and respected B2B media company in any market. (This was the way it was written.)

I want to be the most effective, valued, and respected B2B media company in every market. (This is lots better, don't you think?)

**Any more vs. anymore.** *Anymore* (as one word) is an adverb that means any longer or nowadays. *Any more* (as two words) refers to an additional amount: we don't need any more apples.

**App.** Short for *application program.* Don't capitalize.

**Append vs. upend**. *Append* means to add (at the end), while *upend* means to set on end (a barrel) or to upset (an opinion).

**Appose vs. oppose**. *Appose* means to place (something) side-by-side with another thing, while *oppose* means to stand against, to hinder, obstruct, combat.

**Appraise vs. apprise**. *Apprise* means to inform or give notice of something, while *appraise* means to estimate the value, quality, importance of something.

**Around, 'round, round**. *'Round* is the contraction of *around. Round* means a circular shape. Examples:

I don't want him coming around.

She'll be coming 'round the mountain when she comes.

Our dining room table is round, which I prefer.

**As, because, since.** Each of these words can be used as a conjunction. *As*, however, is a very wimpy conjunction, only implying a relationship between two things, while *since* is a little stronger (suggesting a cause-and-effect relationship), and *because* is the strongest (direct cause-effect relationship).

*As* also means "when," and *since* can mean "from the time that," so be careful when and where you use *as* and *since.*

**Assay vs. essay**. If you *assay* something (like a metal sample) you test it, if you *essay* something you attempt to do it.

**Assent vs. ascent**. *Assent* refers to an agreement, while *ascent* refers to a climb: Our ascent seemed to take forever.

**Attain vs. obtain.** Even though these words are very similar in meaning, they are not synonymous. You'd use *attain* more in the sense of aspire, referring to achievement, accomplishment, to getting something that required sustained effort or time and without outright purchase, something, in general, that can't be taken away: you attain a college degree, you attain your majority, you attain what you set out to do, you attain a certain stature. *Obtain*, on the other hand, is more in the line of acquire, and means to get something through effort, yes, but also by purchase, and, generally, what you obtain can be taken away; for example, you can't attain a diamond ring, but you can obtain one.

**Aver vs. avow.** My mother asked me to include this entry, so I did. There is not a lot of difference between these two words, since both basically mean *to declare*. *Aver* has legalistic overtones, and *avow* (an avowal of love) is very poetic. It is difficult to imagine either of these words being used much in everyday chit chat.

**Awesome.** God is awesome. Mother Nature is awesome. Nothing else makes the cut.

**Back up vs. backup.** *Back up* is the verb; *backup* is the noun and adjective.

**Bail vs. bale**. To *bail* means to remove water from a boat or to post a bond, while *bale* means to secure with wire or cord. Fowler's *A Dictionary of Modern English Usage* suggests that the spelling for jumping from a plane should be bale, as in to "bale out," which is not surprising, given its British bent, but others disagree.

**Bait vs. bate**. *Bate* means to lessen, to restrain ("bated breath"), while *bait* is a lure ("bait the hook").

**Baloney vs. bologna**. *Baloney* a polite term for a lie, and *bologna* is a luncheon meat. But you knew that already, didn't you?

**Bare vs. bear.** The verb *to bare* means to strip, to come clean, to "bare it all." *Bear* as a verb is very versatile. It can mean to hold up, to support. To bear can also mean to give birth, to bring forth, to produce. To bear is used to indicate direction: to bear to the left. There are many popular idiomatic verb phrases associated with bear: to bear up, to bear down, to bear out, and to bear with. A bear, of course, is an animal.

**Bazaar vs. bizarre**. A *bazaar* is an open-air market with many vendors and exotic sounds and smells, while *bizarre* means not just strange, but very strange.

**Beside vs. besides.** *Beside* means next to something; it is a physical location. *Besides* means in addition to something else.

**Better vs. bettor.** A *bettor* is a person who gambles. A *better* is someone who is (or considers him- or herself to be) a person with more status than someone else; in this use, better is almost always plural, as in "He needs to defer to his betters."

**Bi- and semi-.** The prefix *semi-* means twice, as in semiannual (twice a year) and semiweekly (twice a week). The prefix *bi-* means every other, so biannual means every other year, and biweekly means every other week.

**Blanch vs. blench**. Both these words are verbs, but to *blench* is an intransitive verb (which means it does not take an object) that means to shrink away from something/someone (generally in horror), to turn pale (in fear), while to *blanch* is a transitive verb (takes an object) that means to bleach, to whiten, and is commonly used in cooking, and means to scald briefly and then drain.

**Bloc vs. block.** It's voting *bloc*, not voting *block*.

**Blond vs. blonde.** *Blond* is the adjective that describes men with blond hair and people who are blond in general, but the noun *blonde* refers to a woman with blond hair.

**Boor vs. bore.** A *boor* is a person with little or no manners, while a *bore* is someone who repeats uninteresting information. It is certainly possible to be both. Boor is pronounced *boo* with an "r" sound at the end, but bore is pronounced *ore* with a "b" at the beginning; it's subtle, but it's there.

**Born vs. borne**. *Born* refers to birth, while *borne* means tolerated, endured, sustained: "'By God, Scarlett, it isn't to be borne! And it won't be borne!'"—Margaret Mitchell, *Gone With the Wind*. Borne is also used to indicate delivery. When using either word to create a compound adjective, there is disagreement whether or not the created word is one word, two words, or hyphenated: airborne, food borne, blood-borne, firstborn, Southern-born. The solution is to consult a dictionary and use the preferred spelling. Plus, don't forget, whether you use a hyphen or not can depend on a compound adjective's placement in your sentence: before the noun, hyphen; after the noun, no hyphen.

**Breakdown.** One word as a noun; two words as a verb.

**Breakout.** One word as a noun and adjective; two as a verb.

**Breakthrough**. One word as a noun and adjective; two as a verb.

**Breath, breathe, breadth**. *Breath* is what you *breathe*. *Breadth* means width, and oftentimes means freedom from restraint, generosity, something seemingly without limit: the depth and breadth of the ocean.

**Bring vs. take**. *Bring* means to move something towards a fixed point (typically the speaker or writer), while *take* means to move something away from a fixed point.

**Buzzword** is one word.

**C-suite (or C-level)** is a new term that refers to the top of the corporate hierarchy: the CEO, the CFO, the COO, and the CIO.

**Caliber vs. caliper**. *Caliber* is used to refer to the size of bullets a weapon fires: a .44-caliber gun. Caliber can also refer to quality. *Caliper* refers to thickness or depth: a 2-inch caliper oak tree; calipers are the instrument which measures thickness.

**Callous vs. callus**. A *callus* (noun) refers to skin thickened by rough use, while *callous* (adjective) means wanton disregard, insensitivity.

**Canon vs. cannon**. A *cannon* is a weapon, and a *canon* is a principle or standard (the canons of proper etiquette) and often used in reference to religious rules.

**Cant vs. can't.** *Can't*, of course, is the contraction of cannot. *Cant* means pretentious, oftentimes insincere sayings regarding morality or religion.

**Canvas vs. canvass**. To *canvass* means to take a survey, while *canvas* is a type of woven cloth.

**Capital vs. capitol**. A *capital* is the location of the head of government, and it can also mean wealth, first-rate, and an uppercase letter. *Capitol* is used almost exclusively to refer to the building in which the government (state or national) is housed.

**Carat, carrot, karat**. A *carrot* is a vegetable, while *carat* and *karat* are weights: diamonds are measured in carats (a 10-carat pear), and gold is measured in karats (a 14-karat white gold setting).

**CD.** Capitalize. Plural: CDs.

**Cede, concede, secede.** *Cede* means to formally surrender and is often used in the context of territory. *Secede* means to formally withdraw from an association, and *concede* means to acknowledge, to admit.

**Cell phone.** Two words.

**Cite, sight, site**. When you *cite* something written by someone else, you are using his or her opinion/authority to buttress your own writing. A *site* is a place, a location, whether a physical place or—as has become common—a location on the internet. *Sight*, as we all know, is generally used to describe the fact of seeing or what is seen, though sight also can describe the sight of a gun or used in the context of navigation.

**Chafe vs. chaff**. *Chafe* is a verb that means to annoy, irritate, abrade, while *chaff* (a noun) is the leftover portion after wheat or other grain has been threshed (to separate the wheat from the chaff). Chaff is also a military term for metal strips ejected from a plane or ship designed to confuse enemy radar.

**Cheat sheet.** Two words.

**Choose vs. chose.** Like lose and loose, mistakenly using *choose* for *chose* and vice versa is easy to do and difficult to pick up in an edit. *Chose* rhymes with *pose*, and *choose* is pronounced *chews*; choose means to pick, to select, and chose is the past tense of choose: I choose you now. I chose you yesterday. I will choose you soon.

**Chord, cord, cored.** Three homonyms. Let's get *cored* out of the way immediately: cored is the past tense of the verb core. Now, this is the really interesting part. *Cord* is used in the sense of binding, like twine or string: electrical cords. Cord also means ribbed, as in corduroy. Cord is the spelling for anatomical uses: vocal cord, spinal cord, umbilical cord. *Chord* is emotion: His music touched a chord in her heart. Speaking of music, a chord is three musical notes played simultaneously. Chord is the spelling for use in mathematics and aviation.

**Cleave**. *Cleave* is one of those rare words with definitions that mean the exact opposite of one another. Cleave can mean to "cleave into" two or more pieces, to be cut in parts, or it can mean to "cleave together." Interesting. The past tense of cleave is *cleft.*

**Clemson**. What? You don't see the "p"? It's pronounced Clemp' son, not Clem' son. The "p" is invisible. While we're on the subject, Amherst, as in the college, is correctly pronounced with a silent "h," which means, of course, that the "h" isn't pronounced at all. Now you know.

**Climactic vs. climatic**. *Climatic* refers to issues about weather (climate), while *climactic* refers to the climax of an event: The climactic moment in the movie was when Rhett walked out.

**Close-up.** Hyphenate both noun and adjective.

**COD.** Cash on delivery. *COD* is fine, while AP likes *c.o.d.*, but never *cod*, which is a fish.

**Cofound, cofounder.** One word.

**Collage vs. college**. What a difference a vowel makes!

**Collide vs. collision.** Two or more things must be in motion before they can *collide,* but one thing in motion can have a *collision* with a stationary object.

**Complacent vs. complaisant**. *Complacent* means to be smugly satisfied with your ability, while *complaisant* means to be obliging, agreeable.

**Complement vs. compliment**. Distinguishing between these two words is a real problem for many people. A *compliment* is an expression of praise; *complimentary* means something given at no cost. *Complement* can be used when two things are brought together and the second thing is compatible with or completes the first: The kitchen cabinets complemented the countertops. Complement also can mean completeness of a workforce: The casino quickly hired its full complement of blackjack dealers.

My memory hooks are simple. *I* compliment you (*compliment* with an I); *I* am paying for lunch (compliment with an I). If something "completes" something else, why, that is complement (complete ends in an E) with an E.

**Compose vs. comprise.** A thing is *composed* of individual parts; individual parts *comprise* a larger thing. A team is composed of members; individual members comprise a team. A jury is composed of jurors and a foreman; citizens comprise a jury. Never write "comprised of." This is incorrect: Florida courts are comprised of 20 judicial circuits.

**Confidant vs. confident**. A *confidant* is someone you confide in, while *confident* is to be assured of a certain outcome: She was confident her confidant would keep her secret.

**Connote vs. denote.** *Connote* means to suggest or imply a meaning in addition to some other word: Pineapples connote hospitality. *Denote* means to specify or to mean: Her behavior in buying the Porsche 918 denotes a certain *joie de vivre.*

**Conscience vs. conscious**. A *conscience* tells us right from wrong, while being *conscious* is the state of awareness: He was conscious of his conscience as he made his decision.

**Continual vs. continuous.** Though some style guides say that there is no difference between these two words, I disagree. *Continuous* means unceasing, constant, uninterrupted, while *continual* means frequent and regular, in the sense of intermittent.

**Copy-edit.** That, as a verb, according to *The New York Times Manual of Style and Usage.* But, copy editor.

**Could.** The expression is *couldn't care less*, not *could care less.*

**Council vs. counsel**. A *council* is a group of advisers; to *counsel* someone is to give that person advice: His council of councilors counseled him to beware of trying too hard.

**Coup vs. coupe**. A *coupe* (also coupé) is a two-door car, while a *coup* is a sudden, successful act (a coup d'état).

**Couple.** When referring to two people, use a plural verb and pronoun, e.g., The couple were asked to leave. When referring to two people as a unit, use a singular verb and pronoun: The newly married couple was toasted all night. (Um, wait a minute; perhaps a rephrasing is necessary here!)

**Couple of.** The expression is *a couple of,* and it takes a plural verb: A couple [of them] were refused service.

**Cover up.** No hyphen as a verb; hyphenated as noun and adjective.

**Credible, creditable, credulous**. *Credible* means believable, trustworthy. *Creditable* means worthy of credit. *Credulous* means gullible.

**Cutting-edge.** Hyphenated as an adjective, but not as a verb or noun.

**Dais, lectern, podium, pulpit.** A *dais* (day' ess) is a large raised platform for more than one person (think "stage") built to accommodate a throne or lectern. A *podium* is a small platform built for one person (think "soapbox") on which a speaker or an athlete stands. A *lectern* is a stand with (most times) a tilted place for a speaker's notes. A lectern *is not* a podium. You step up onto a dais or a podium; you stand behind (or next to or in front of) a lectern. A *pulpit* is a lectern (often on a podium) for ministers.

**Data.** Data is a plural noun and is used with a plural verb.

**Decent, descent, dissent.** *Decent* means okay, good or worthy: He's a decent enough guy. A *descent* (from the verb *descend*) is the pathway from a high place, while to *dissent* means to disagree and is often used in a philosophical or religious context.

**Defuse vs. diffuse**. *Defuse* means to make less violent, as in: He defused the volatile situation. *Diffuse* means to spread out, especially in a liquid or gaseous sense: The acrid smoke became more diffuse as the wind strengthened.

**Demur vs. demure.** To *demur* is to object, generally because of moral or religious scruples: They asked me to be president, but I demurred because I felt I was too new of a member. *Demure* means modest, shy, reserved.

**Dent vs. dint**. The expression "by *dint* of" refers to the results of effort, power, or force, while a *dent* refers to divot-type damage to a surface.

**Desert vs. dessert.** She ate a chocolate *dessert* in the barren *desert*. Watch that extra "s."

**Desperate vs. disparate**. *Disparate* means dissimilar, and is often used in the context of choice: a disparate group of candidates. *Desperate* means having little hope or an anxious need (or both).

**Deter vs. detour.** To *deter* is to discourage, restrain, prevent. To *detour* is to avoid, to go around; a *detour* is an alternate route.

**Device vs. devise**. A *device* is a noun and means something that helps or assists. A dishwasher is a device that helps wash dishes; a lie is a device that helps you get out of trouble (sometimes). *Devise* is a verb, and means to invent, construct, or plan.

**Different**. The expression is always *different from*, never *different than*.

**Difficult, hard, tough.** These words do have some overlap of meaning, but they are not completely interchangeable. In formal writing, I would consign *hard* to uses that involve stones and rocks, *tough* to inanimate things, and *difficult* to what humans experience when, for example, they try to learn something new, like playing the piano.

**Disburse, dispense, disperse.** *Disburse* means to pay out; *dispense* means to distribute, to do away with, or to give away; and *disperse* means to scatter.

He disbursed his fortune to his creditors.

An ATM dispenses money.

The leaves were dispersed by the gale.

**Disinterested vs. uninterested.** *Uninterested* means indifferent, bored, while *disinterested* means not influenced by selfish motives, unbiased, impartial.

**Disc vs. disk.** Use *disk* with medical and computer references, while *disc* should be used when referring to phonographic records and related terms.

**Discreet vs. discrete**. *Discreet* means avoiding gossip, being prudent and circumspect, while *discrete* means apart, separate, distinct, individual. *Indiscreet* means imprudent.

**Disillusion vs. dissolution.** To *disillusion* someone is to make that person give up his or her fantasies, while *dissolution* is the act of dissolving.

**Dot-com.** Hyphenated. Reference to an internet-based business.

**Double-.** The prefix *double-* is hyphenated in all uses as an adjective and a verb, but only sometimes as noun: double-check, double-play, double-dribble, double-knit, double-jointed, double-space, double-speak, double-decker, double-cross, and so on. As a noun, the use is almost always two words: double fault, double jeopardy, double feature, double play, double cross, double entendre. When in doubt, double-check.

**Draft vs. draught**. *Draft*, of course, can be a verb (to draft an opinion) or can be a noun (pour me a draft [of beer], or, feel that draft [of air]), and also can be used as an adjective (a draft horse), but *draught*—which is a British word and is pronounced just like "draft" and not like "taught"—means the depth of water necessary to float a ship. It can also be used in its plural form (draughts) as a synonym for the game of checkers. Don't confuse draught with drought.

**DVD.** Capitalize. Plural: DVDs.

**Each vs. apiece**. These two words can be interchangeable in the sense of "The tickets cost $350 apiece/each."

**Each other vs. one another**. Some people opine that *one another* should refer to more than two people, and *each other* should refer to two people, but, when push comes to shove, according to Fowler's *A Dictionary of Modern English Usage*, they are interchangeable. The possessive of each other is each other's, never each others'.

**Earth.** Capitalize when referring to our planet (the Earth is my home); lowercase when a state of mind: After his euphoria ebbed, he returned to earth.

**Eldest vs. oldest**. The *oldest* child in a family is the *eldest.*

**Elegy vs. eulogy.** An *elegy* is a mournful lament, whether spoken or sung, while a *eulogy* is a speech in praise of someone, and is generally recognized as the speech about the recently deceased at that person's funeral. "Elegiac" is a real "*New York Times* word."

**Elicit vs. illicit**. *Elicit* means to bring forth (his assertion elicited general laughter), while *illicit* refers to behavior or something (e.g., a drug) that is immoral or illegal.

**Eminent, immanent, imminent**. *Imminent* means impending, likely to occur at any moment, while *eminent* means prominent, distinguished, conspicuous. *Immanent* means innate, indwelling, remaining within, inherent. *Preeminent* means superior.

**Empathize vs. emphasize**. *Empathize* means to identify with another person's feelings or situation, while *emphasize* means to highlight or stress.

**Enervate vs. innervate.** To *enervate* means to weaken, while to *innervate* means to stimulate, to invigorate.

**Enquiry vs. inquiry.** Use *inquiry*, unless you are British.

**Eon vs. ion**. An *ion* is a charged particle, and an *eon* is a really, really long time.

**Every day vs. everyday**. *Everyday* is an adjective that means daily, commonplace, ordinary: an everyday occurrence, an everyday dress. *Every day* refers to time, and means something that happens regularly or each day: Take one pill every day.

**Evoke vs. invoke**. *Evoke* means to bring up (as in stirred up), to elicit, especially emotions or imagery, while *invoke* means to call upon, usually for aid.

**Exhort vs. extort.** To *extort* means to take money by intimidating someone, while to *exhort* means to urge someone to do something: He exhorted her to make a greater effort.

**Explicit vs. implicit**. *Explicit* means precise, obvious, while *implicit* means implied.

**Faint vs. feint**. When someone *faints* he or she loses consciousness temporarily. A *feint* (usually in a fight or a battle) is a strategic move designed to mislead an opponent. A related word is feign, which means to pretend.

**Fair vs. fare.** This would be a very easy typo to make. *Fair* means just, beautiful. A *fair* is also similar to an amusement park, but with leavening "exhibits" of art work, crafts, plants, and animals. A *fare* is a payment, usually for some sort of transportation. It can also mean outcome, as in "How did you fare at the competition?"

**Farther vs. further**. *Farther* refers to a precise distance; *further* means more: think "far" to help you distinguish between farther and further.

Farther is an adjective and adverb that means to or at a more distant point, to move away. Use only in conjunction with a precise distance.

Examples:

We rode fifty-five miles today; tomorrow, we will ride fifty miles farther.

Further is an adjective and adverb and means an extension of time or at a greater extent or degree, in the sense of "more": I need to understand the issue a little better before I can discuss it further. It also means more distance, but not a precise distance.

Examples:

We had to travel further than we thought we would.

Please move us further from the door.

Please move us further away from the door.

Further can also mean "in addition": The Presidential Parkway protesters further demanded the wholesale cutting of the trees be halted until the court decided the issue.

**FAQs.** The plural form of this acronym is appropriate.

**Faze vs. phase.** I thought these words could be included in the homonym list (who could mistake one for the other?), but I just finished picking up my jaw from the floor at seeing a HuffPo editor use "phase" for "faze." *Faze* means to disturb or to slow down: It didn't faze me. *Phase* means a certain period of time or a part of a larger whole: He reacts to the phase of the moon; He's going through a phase; In this phase of the investigation, we just don't know.

**Fewer vs. less.** *Less* refers to concepts that can't be quantified; *fewer*, on the other hand, refers to things that can be counted. Use fewer, not less, when something refers to a number, something you can count, rather than an amount. Remember: fewer snowflakes, less snow. This is incorrect:

Less than one-half of one percent (0.5%) of active attorneys in the United States will ever receive this honor.

So, yes, a sign that says "10 Items or Less" is grammatically incorrect.

**Flounder vs. founder.** A *flounder* (noun) is a flat, bottom-feeding fish. To *flounder* (verb) is to stagger or struggle, whether physically, in mud or water, financially (my company floundered in the bad economy), or mentally. To *founder* (verb) means to fill with water and sink, to fail or break down, as well as to become ill from overeating. To founder also means to become lame (as in horses). Founder (noun) also refers to the person or persons who started an enterprise: She is among the original founders of the bank.

**Flair vs. flare**. *Flair* means noticeable talent, while a *flare* is what you send up when you are in trouble at sea. The expression "flare up" means to suddenly become worse: His arthritis flared up and he was miserable.

**Flier vs. flyer**. A *flier* is another word for aviator. There is disagreement whether *flyer* or flier is best when referring to a circular or a handbill: flyer seems to have won out, but flier has its adherents.

**Florescence vs. fluorescence.** *Florescence* is the act of blooming, of flowering, while *fluorescence* describes the light emitted by a substance during radiation.

**Forego vs. forgo**. To *forgo* means to abstain from something. *Forego* means to go before, as in a "foregone conclusion."

**Foreword vs. forward**. A *foreword* is an introduction to a book, written by someone other than the author. *Forward* means to advance, to move toward the front.

**Frontline, frontlines.** One word as an adjective (a frontline view) and a noun as a plural, but I prefer "front line" as a singular noun: He found himself at the front line of the battle. (Do you *hear* the difference?)

**Fundraiser, fundraising.** Always one word.

**Gage vs. gauge.** Chances are that you'll never use the word *gage*, which is something (like a glove) that a knight would throw down to indicate he was issuing a challenge. Gage can also mean something given as a pledge. *Gauge* is both a verb and a noun. As a verb, gauge means to measure, to judge; as a noun, a gauge is a device used for measuring.

**Gait vs. gate**. *Gait* refers to movement (a horse's gait, an uneven gait), while a *gate* is a barrier that swings open and shut.

**Gen X.** Short for Generation X, referring to people born after 1965. No hyphen as a noun, but hyphenated as an adjective: Gen Xer, Gen-X crowd, according to *The New York Times*. Don't forget that *generation* is a collective noun, so Generation X is as well.

**Go.** "Go" is not synonymous with "said." You'd never (I hope) say: "And then, she goes 'I hate you!'!" Please don't "go" there.

**Guesswork.** one word.

**Guys.** A "guy" is a man, usually a young man. "You 'guys'" should never be used to address a group of men and women, especially men and women older than 18. Oh, honey, don't get me started.

**Hail vs. hale.** *Hail* means icy pellets (memory hook: there's an "i" in hail and an "i" in ice) and to raise your hand/arm to recognize someone, as in to "hail the Queen." *Hale* means healthy, and is usually joined as a phrase: to be "hale and hearty."

**Hairy vs. harry**. *Hairy* means hair-covered (or, as a slang term, crazy or weird), while *harry* (a verb) means to stalk or harass.

**Hallmark vs. trademark.** A *hallmark* refers to general details describing a group: A nose for scandal is the hallmark of a good gossip columnist. A *trademark* is a detail or details describing a specific person or thing. "Trademark" is also a legal process used by a manufacturer to distinguish its unique goods from another's.

**Hands down.** No hyphen, no apostrophe. In fact, none of the "hands" expressions, like hand in hand, hand to mouth, hand it to, hand in glove, or hand over fist, use hyphens.

**Hangar vs. hanger**. You store clothes on a *hanger*; you store planes in a *hangar*.

**Hang vs. hung**. I will *hang* the painting and then it will be *hung*; the murderer was *hanged*.

**Hard vs. difficult**. Though *hard* is often used to describe a degree of *difficulty*, the word is best used to describe a state of being, e.g., The stone was hard.

**Hard core.** As an adjective following the noun, two words; as an adjective preceding the noun, hyphenated: the team's fan base was hard core; a hard-core fan base.

**Hardy vs. hearty.** *Hardy* means tough, while *hearty* means enthusiastic.

**Have, half, halve**. *Have* is a verb meaning to possess: I have his number. *Half* means to divide something into two equal parts, while *halve* is the verb that lets you do it.

I have to halve this pie into two parts; I will give you one half and keep the other for myself.

Halves is the plural of half: I need two pounds of pecan halves for my deep-dish pecan-tangerine pie.

Note: halfway is one word.

**Head shot vs. headshot.** A head shot will ruin a great headshot.

**Heads up.** No hyphen when used as an interjection: Hey! *Heads up*! But, use a hyphen with both noun and adjective use: he gave her a *heads-up*; that was a *heads-up* play.

**Hence, henceforth, hither, thence, thither, whence**. All these words mean "from," whether "from" a place, origin, or cause. *Hence* can mean "for this reason" and "therefore." Hence and *henceforth* can also be used to illustrate time, whether in the sense of "at this exact moment" or at some time in the future:

At some point hence, we'll understand what she said.

Henceforth, all okra shall be banned.

*Whence* means "from a place": Go back to the shadow from whence you came.

Whence is not to be confused with *wince, wither, weather,* or *whether,* which are words that sound the same or similar but have meanings completely different from the concept of "from."

**High-five.** Always hyphenated.

**Historically vs. traditionally**. *Traditionally* means customary, established, conventional, while *historically* means documented, authentic, factual, attested.

**Hit-and-run.** Hyphens as a noun and adjective; no hyphens as a verb.

**Home vs. hone.** To *hone* (verb) means to sharpen (to hone a knife) or to improve, to perfect, as in a skill. To *home in on* (verb phrase) something means to return to or to get closer to: The missile homed in on its target.

**Home town vs. hometown.** In the two-word use, "home" is an adjective modifying "town": Brunswick is my home town. "Hometown" as one word is also an adjective: He is a hometown hero.

**How-to.** Hyphenated as a noun and adjective; plural: how-tos.

**Ignominy.** I include this only because it's given me fits for forever. *Ignominy* means public shame or embarrassment, and it's pronounced **ig'** nah min ee.

**Impede vs. impinge.** *Impede* is a transitive verb that means to obstruct, to hinder, while *impinge,* an intransitive verb, means to encroach, to infringe (usually followed by *on*).

**Imply vs. infer.** Words *imply* what a listener *infers.*

**In-depth.** Hyphenated in all uses.

**In-house.** Hyphenated in all uses.

**Incite vs. insight**. To *incite* (a fight, a riot, an insurrection) means to trigger (usually violence), while gaining *insight* into something is to gain understanding about that person or thing.

**Inevitable vs. invariable.** Though these words have a somewhat overlapping meaning, they are not quite the same. *Invariable* means unchanging, static, while *inevitable* means unavoidable, inescapable, certain.

**Indict vs. indite.** While both words are pronounced in DITE. i*ndict* means "to charge someone with a crime," and *indite* means "to write, compose, dictate."

**Ingenious vs. ingenuous**. *Ingenious* means brilliant, as in super smart, while *ingenuous* means straightforward, candid, artless. *Disingenuous* (some dictionaries use a hyphen), then, means hypocritical, insincere.

**Inherent vs. inherit**. *Inherent* means a fundamental characteristic, while *inherit* means to be given something (blue eyes, a Porsche 911 in Amethyst Metallic) by someone else.

**Insure, assure, ensure**. Distinguishing between insure and ensure is a real problem for many people. *Insure* should only be used in the context of insurance, while *ensure* means to make sure or certain. I once saw "insure" used for "ensure" in a lawyer's text—a lawyer who billed *$1800 per hour*. *Assure* means to give confidence, which I assuredly did not have with that lawyer.

**Iteration vs. reiteration.** *Iteration* is a noun and means a previously created example, version, incarnation: That iteration of my speech was the best so far. *Reiteration* is a verb, and refers to the physical act of repetition, as in, "Let me reiterate: you are wrong, wrong, wrong!"

**It's vs. its**. This is such a common error that it is worth repeating: *It's* is not the possessive of *it is*, it's the contraction of *it is*. *Its* is the possessive of *it is*: NO APOSTROPHE. It would be worthwhile to do a document search prior to publication and review every single *its* and *it's*, just to be on the safe side.

**JPEG, JPG, .jpg.** These are all acceptable. Just be consistent.

**Keynote.** One word.

**Kick off vs. kickoff.** Verb form two words; one word as noun.

**Kudos.** Despite appearances, *kudos* is a singular noun.

**Lead vs. led.** This can be tricky. *Lead* is a verb that is pronounced *leed,* and means to guide, to influence. *Led*, which is pronounced led, is the past tense of lead. *Lead* is also a metal, and is pronounced led.

**Lend vs. loan**. Lend (verb) vs. loan (noun). Although some people feel *loan* should only be used as a noun, lend and loan are both acceptable as verbs in standard English: "Can you *lend* (loan) me a dollar?" A person or entity that loans money is a lender, not a loaner. However, only lend should be used in a figurative sense: "Can you lend me a hand?"

**Lessen vs. lesson**. We all know the difference between these two words, but they are so similar that a "search" prior to publication might be worthwhile.

**Libel vs. slander**. To *libel* someone is to print mean things about that person, while to *slander* someone is to say mean things about that person. Gossip, for example, is slander, if it's not true. Whether or not what's said is true, of course, is sometimes open to interpretation.

**Lie vs. lay**. Lay (lay, laid, laid, laying) and lie (lie, lay, lain, lying) are often used synonymously. *Lay* is a transitive verb, meaning that it takes an object. (See also Shined vs. shone.) To "lay something" means to place something somewhere. *Lie*, on the other hand, is intransitive and means to recline. The distinction between these related verbs is further blurred by the fact that past tense of lie is lay. An easy rule of thumb is to replace the words with sit and set. If sit makes sense (to sit down) then lie should be used (to lie down). If the sentence works with set (e.g., set the papers on the desk) then lay should be used (lay the papers on the desk). A layoff is never a lieoff or lyoff. (To lie can also mean "to not tell the truth"—but, in that case, the past tense is lied.) Go slow with this because it can really trip you up.

**Lifelong.** One word.

**Lifestyle.** Trending to one word as both a noun and an adjective.

**Lightening vs. lightning.** Be careful here. *Lightening* (to lighten, a verb) means to make less heavy, less dark, to brighten: She lightened her hair. *Lightning* (noun) is the electric spark inside thunderclouds or, as an adjective, means to move swiftly.

**Lineage vs. linage.** *Lineage* refers to ancestral heritage: according to Luke, Joseph was "of the house and lineage of David." *Linage* refers to the number of printed lines, in an advertisement, for example, or in a newspaper story.

**Loath vs. loathe**. *Loath* means reluctant (I was loath to correct him), while to *loathe* something or someone indicates a serious dislike.

**Log in.** No hyphen as a verb; one word a noun.

**Lose vs. loose.** I see confusion about which [one] of these two words is correct all too often: to *lose* means to misplace, while *loose* means not tight (to loosen means to make less tight, less binding). This is a mistake that's easy to make, but difficult to see.

**Make up, make-up, makeup.** One word as a noun; two as a verb; hyphenated as an adjective preceding its noun.

**Man-to-man.** Hyphenated as an adjective before the modified noun: a man-to-man talk, man-to-man coverage.

**Manor vs. manner**. Manner refers to behavior; manners refers to methods of social interaction (polite or not). A manor is a large estate, typically with surrounding acreage. The popular phrase "to the manner born" (no, it's not "manor") is from *Hamlet.*

**Many vs. much.** In general, the main uses of both *many* and *much* can be articulated as follows: use *many* to describe things that be counted (many books), and *much* to describe things that can't (much learning), just like *fewer* and *less.*

**May be vs. maybe.** Watch that space! Isn't it interesting: *maybe* expresses doubt (Maybe it's true that...), while *may be* can express certainty (While that very well may be the truth...).

**Millennial.** Capitalize only when referring to people born in the '80s and '90s: a Millennial, the Millennials. This is contrary to style at *The New York Times*, but it makes sense.

**Mindset.** One word. It's one of those new words.

**Mix up.** No hyphen with the verb; hyphenate noun and adjective.

**Mock-up.** Hyphenated noun.

**Naval vs. navel**. *Naval* is a reference to a navy, while *navel* refers to a bellybutton and a variety of seedless orange.

**Neither/nor**. Neither/nor with two singular parts is singular. Example: Neither the mother nor the daughter was considered particularly handsome. (Neither one was considered particularly handsome. Not "were.") Same thing goes with either/or.

**Nod vs. shake.** To *nod* your head (up and down) generally indicates agreement; to *shake* your head (from side to side) generally indicates disagreement. Shake also means vigorous, yet irregular movement: to mix.

**None.** *None* is the source of huge controversy, but the fact of the matter is that H. W. Fowler's *A Dictionary of Modern English Usage* states that *none* is more commonly used to indicate more than one thing, and so takes a plural verb, as in "None [of them] are tired." If, however, you are using *none* in the sense of *no one* or *not one* (none of it was useful), then it would take a singular verb; however, why not use *no one* or *not one* instead? Note: nonetheless is one word.

**Nonprofit.** One word. However, **for-profit** and **not-for-profit**, with hyphens.

**Odor vs. ordure.** *Odor* means smell, while *ordure* means manure: The odor of the ordure was awful.

**Offer vs. proffer.** There is very little, if any, substantive difference between these two words, though *proffer* is much more formal and "literary."

**Offline.** One word.

**OK, O.K., okay**. Each of these is acceptable, though the *AP Stylebook* nixes *okay* (which lots of people like). *OK* is a computer command. The *New York Times* columnist Paul Krugman recently used *O.K.* It's never spelled ok or Ok. Just be consistent and you'll be okay.

**On to vs. onto.** I was just uploading this manuscript and found myself staring at the following sentence:

You should address all the errors and warnings before moving onto the cover step. (Sentence compliments of CreateSpace.)

*Stop the presses,* I thought. *No way. You can't take a physical position on a place called "the cover step."* H. W. Fowler is somewhat difficult on this issue (ha!), but seems to be saying that you should use *onto* (a one-word preposition) when you can use *on* (also a preposition), but use *on to* (two words: an adverb plus preposition) when you can't. Another hint that this sentence is incorrect is that the expression is "move on," which helps separate the two words: on to. *Chicago* says that the way to be sure is to insert "up" and make the phrase *up on to*; if that works, use onto.

Bottom line: I did "stop the presses" and did a search of this entire manuscript for onto and on to, just to make sure. Didn't find anything, but...*phew*! That's a sneaky son of a gun.

**One-time vs. onetime.** *One-time* means once, while *onetime* means former.

**Onset vs. outset**. *Onset* means the beginning or start (of a disease, an attack, etc.) of a situation or event which will have some duration, while *outset* refers to the starting moment. (Outset is sometimes shown as two words or with a hyphen, but the one-word usage is most proper.)

**Opt-in, opt-out.** Hyphened as nouns, but no hyphens as verbs.

**Ordinance vs. ordnance**. An *ordinance* is a governmental rule, while *ordnance* refers to artillery and ammunition.

**Over all vs. overall.** A pair of *overalls* is an item of clothing worn by farmers and mechanics (and others) to protect clothing underneath; *over all* (two words) is an adverb.

**Overrule vs. reverse.** This is a legalistic difference: the Supreme Court *reverses* the decisions of lower courts, while lower courts can *overrule* their own decisions or the decisions of other, lower courts.

**Paean vs. peon.** A *paean* is a song of praise, while a *peon* is someone from the lower classes, a member of the hoi polloi.

**Palette, palate, pallet, epaulette**. An artist's *palette* of paints, a gourmand's fussy *palate*, a heavy *pallet* of bricks. *Epaulettes* are ornamental shoulder pieces—sometimes gold, with braids—worn on a military-style jacket.

**Parallel vs. tandem.** *Parallel* means two things that are side by side but do not touch, though the two things may be similar or identical (my thoughts paralleled his). *Tandem* refers to two connected things where one is following the other (they rode a tandem bicycle).

**Parameter vs. perimeter**. Think about a circle. *Parameter* means to the limit, to the edge, and encompasses the interior: the parameters of the policy. *Perimeter* means the outer border or boundary line alone, and does not include the interior.

**Past vs. passed**. The *past* refers to a time before the present, while *passed* refers to something that moved near and then ahead of something else (my Alfa Romeo passed his Porsche on the highway), or issues from one thing and travels to another (he passed the ball).

**Peek, peak, pique**. *Peek* is a verb that means to look at quickly, to glance, while *peak* means the apex, zenith, uppermost, and *pique* means to be annoyed (a fit of pique) or excited (her interest was piqued).

**Personal vs. personnel**. *Personal* refers to a situation, event, or person that directly affects a particular person, while *personnel* refer (note the plural verb) to people employed by an organization.

**Perspective vs. prospective**. *Prospective* means possible in the future: the prospective student, the prospective player, something that someone hopes will become reality—think "prospect." *Perspective* refers to point of view: From my perspective he is the perfect prospective husband.

**Physical vs. psychical**. *Psychical* means "pertaining to the human soul or mind," while *physical* refers to the material body.

**Piano.** Plural: pianos.

**Pick up.** Two words as a verb, one word as a noun, and hyphenated as an adjective.

**Pigeonhole.** One word, as both noun and verb.

**Pile up.** Two words as a verb, one as noun and adjective.

**Pixilated vs. pixelated**. *Pixilated* means affected by fairies, eccentric, fanciful, while *pixelated* means an image with obvious pixels.

**Plaintiff vs. plaintive**. *Plaintive* (adjective) means mournful, while a *plaintiff* (noun) is the party that brings suit in court.

**Play off.** Two words as a verb, one word as a noun, hyphenated as an adjective.

**Pleaded versus pled.** Use *pleaded*. It's always correct.

**Plug-in.** Hyphenated as a noun.

**Point-blank.** Hyphenated expression.

**Politics.** As noun, generally uses a plural verb; as a profession or a hobby, use a singular verb.

**Pooh-pooh.** To speak disparagingly of: He pooh-poohed the idea.

**Pour, poor, pore**. Skin has *pores*, and you gaze intently at something (they pored over the maps), while you *pour* a drink. A person is *poor* if he (or she!) has little money.

**Practicable vs. practical**. *Practicable* means feasible, able to be put into practice, while *practical* means useful.

**Practice vs. practise**. In the States these two words are interchangeable and mean to drill or rehearse, though *practice*, not *practise*, is the word used to describe the work—the practice—of a doctor or a lawyer. The spelling ending in –se is more common in the United Kingdom, so stick with *practice* in the States.

**Pratfall vs. pitfall.** A *pratfall* is an embarrassing fall (on your backside), while a *pitfall* is a trap for the unwary. In British English, a *prat* is a jackass or an incompetent person.

**Pray vs. prey**. *Pray,* of course, means to offer thanks or supplications to a deity, while *prey* either describes the target of a hunter (noun) or, as a verb, means to bother, to disturb, to victimize: She fell prey to her volatile emotions.

**Precede vs. proceed**. *Precede* means something that comes before, like an event, time, rank, or importance. *Proceed* means to move forward, to continue, and, in its plural form (proceeds), can indicate something that happens after or results from something else, such as financial gains or an event.

**Precedence vs. precedent.** A *precedent* (often used in law) is something that happened before and is used as a guide, example, standard, or model, while *precedence* refers to something that comes before something else because the first thing is superior in rank or more important: A gunshot takes precedence over a toothache in an emergency room.

**Precipitate vs. precipitous**. *Precipitous* means dangerously steep; *precipitate* means sudden.

**Premier vs. premiere.** A *premier* (noun) is a governmental position; premier is also a noun, meaning first in rank or first in time. A *premiere* (noun) is the first public performance of a play or movie. Premiere is also a verb: The movie premiered on Monday.

**Preposition vs. proposition**. A *proposition* is the act of suggesting a certain thing be accepted, done, or considered. A *preposition* is a word or phrase that modifies verbs, nouns, or adjectives and expresses a spatial or temporal relationship (*by, at, under, to, in, since, on,* etc.) between the two.

**Prescribe vs. proscribe.** You'd use *prescribe* in relationship to a prescription from a doctor, meaning to dictate a course of action. *Proscribe* means to prohibit, denounce, condemn.

**Principal vs. principle**. *Principal* means someone in a leadership position (the princi*pal* is my *pal*), the main or highest in rank, and for the most part (the principal difference). Principal can also refer to the noninterest portion of a loan. *Principle*, on the other hand, means fundamental rule, precept, rationale.

**Prior vs. previous**. Though these words are nearly synonymous, there is a difference, though it's difficult to put your finger on exactly what it is. *Prior* is often used as prior to, and so refers to an event that immediately precedes another. And, of course, there's no such word as "priorly." Some words just don't "go" with one or the other, so try the other word if one doesn't seem quite right. Priors generally refers to prior convictions.

**Prophecy vs. prophesy.** BEWARE! Wow, these had me fooled! *Prophecy* is the noun: a prediction or foretelling, generally divinely inspired. It is pronounced "**prof** ess see." *Prophesy* is the verb: to predict or foretell, and it is pronounced "**prof** ess eye." The plural of prophecy is prophecies, and the forms of prophesy are prophesies, prophesied, prophesying, and always with the long *I* sound (eye). A reader mispronounced "prophesy" seven (!) times at church last Sunday. Don't do that.

**Prostate vs. prostrate**. Misuse at your peril.

**Province, provenance, providence, provident**. *Province* refers to a geographical area, a field of activity or area of authority. *Provenance* means the source, the origin. *Providence* (usually with a capital P) means the care or guidance of God (e.g., Divine Providence). *Provident* means prudence, careful management.

**Punitive vs. putative.** *Punitive* relates to punishment, as in laws, damages, actions, while *putative* means supposed, reputed, or commonly regarded as being, as in "He was the putative father of the infant."

**Push-button.** Hyphenated as a noun and adjective.

**Q & A.** For Question and Answer session. Q-and-A is acceptable.

**Quarry vs. query.** A *quarry* can be an open excavation where rocks and minerals, like granite, is mined; it can also mean prey: The hunter stalked his clever quarry. To quarry as a verb means the act of mining. *Query* can also be a noun and a verb, and means to question: She queried her professor after class.

**Rack vs. wrack.** A *rack* is a structure or framework to organize or display something; rack also refers to adding additional items (rack up more points). *Wrack* refers to wreckage, as in wrack and ruin, to wrack one's brain.

**Racket vs. racquet.** *Racket* refers to loud noises or a criminal enterprise. *Racquet* refers to a tennis, squash, or badminton racquet. And then, of course, there is "racquetball." The *AP Stylebook* likes "racket" for both uses; however, many tennis (and squash, badminton, and racquetball) players would disagree. In fact, it seems that all people who actually *use* a racquet to play a game prefer that spelling, so, what does AP know?

**Raise vs. raze.** *Raise*, of course, can mean to build up, to elevate; *raze* means to tear down, to bulldoze. Interesting.

**Rank and file.** No hyphens for the noun; hyphens for the adjective: rank-and-file members.

**Rappel vs. repel.** These two words sound so close to the same that I thought I'd let you see what you think: Is there a substantial difference in the way you pronounce *rappel* and *repel*? (Don't let it drive you crazy.) Rappel is a term used by mountain climbers, and means a controlled descent. Repel means to disgust, to push away.

**Rebut vs. refute.** To *rebut* something means to argue against it, but to *refute* something means to prove it wrong.

**Recurring vs. reoccurring**. Though both these words mean events that occur again and again, *recurring* refers to events that happen regularly or predictably, while *reoccurring* refers to events that repeat themselves without predictability or regularity.

**Red-handed.** Hyphenate both noun and adjective.

**Regime vs. regimen**. These words are closely related. In English, *regime* means a system of government, like a monarchy or dictatorship, while *regimen* means to follow a system of living, such as exercise and diet, meant to improve quality of life. In French, to *suivre un régime* means to diet.

**Rein, reign, and rain**. Expressions like "give free *rein*," "check *rein*," and "*rein* in" originated with the concept of guiding a horse. *Reign* refers to a king/queen's reign, and *rain*, of course, refers to wet weather.

**Reprise, reprisal.** To *reprise* means to repeat, while a *reprisal* means to retaliate.

**Restaurateur.** It's *restaurateur*, not restauranteur. Oops!

**Rife, rifle, riffle**. *Rife* means full of something: The manuscript was rife with errors. *Rifle* refers to a type of gun, as well as to ransack, steal, or plunder. *Riffle* means to leaf quickly through pages or cards, whether bound or loose.

**Rigor vs. vigor.** These words are not synonymous. *Rigor* means strictness, severity, austerity, harshness. *Vigor* means drive, force, vitality, strength—with a positive spin that is almost always associated with good health.

**Rip off.** No hyphen as a verb; hyphenate as a noun and adjective.

**Road map.** Two words.

**Room.** Did you ever wonder whether a —room word is one word or two words? Well, here's the trick: for prefix words of one syllable, it's one word (bedroom, bathroom), but, prefix words of two or more syllables create two words (living room, dining room). Now you know.

**Salespeople.** One word.

**Screen saver.** Two words.

**Second guess.** No hyphen as a noun; hyphenate the verb form.

**Second-rate.** Always hyphenated.

**Set up vs. setup.** One word as noun, two words as verb.

**Sew, so, sow**. Since these are real words and are pronounced identically, watch your usage. One does not "sew" discord among one's enemies: one sows discord.

**Shake up.** No hyphen as a verb; hyphenated as noun and adjective.

**Shape up.** No hyphen as a verb; hyphenated as noun and adjective.

**Shear vs. sheer**. To *shear* means to cut (to shear sheep), while *sheer* means thin (the dress was sheer), or sharp (the sheer drop off the cliff), or dramatic (her sheer effrontery). Sheer can also mean unmixed, as in "We tunneled through a mile of sheer rock."

**Shined vs. shone**. The verb shine has two main definitions: a) to emit light (intransitive), and b) to cause to gleam by polishing (transitive). Remember: A transitive verb requires a direct object to receive the action of the verb, as in: I hit the ball. An intransitive verb does not require a direct object, as in: I ran. In other words, the subject is doing the action of the intransitive verb and nothing receives the action. As an intransitive verb, shine makes shone in its past-tense, perfect-tense, and past-participle forms. As a transitive verb, it makes shined. Examples:

A fan at the Georgia-Georgia Tech game was treated at the hospital after a laser pen was shone in his eyes.

His comments shone a light on what was needed to move forward in our marriage.

He was highly polished, right down to his spit-shined shoes; it was clear to me that his position as head of the Animal Services division never brought him out of his office to actually interact with his charges.

They polished the chrome until it shined in the sun.

**Side by side.** No hyphens after modified noun; hyphenated before.

**Sign up.** No hyphen as a verb; hyphenated as noun and adjective.

**Simple vs. simplistic.** *Simple* means easy to understand; lots of times, when something is simple it's a good thing. (You don't, however, want to be simple-minded!) *Simplistic* is not a fancy way of saying simple. In fact, simplistic is a derogatory term, something you'd say to someone who had ignored or glossed over an important element in an argument; for example: It's totally simplistic to say that all pit bulls are bad dogs.

**Sit in.** Not hyphenated as a verb; hyphenate as a noun and adjective.

**Sober vs. somber**. The primary definition of *sober* is "not drunk," but it also can mean subdued, grave, sedate. *Somber* means grave, dismal, gloomy, dull.

**Sneaked vs. snuck**. *Sneaked* is the preferred past tense of sneak, not snuck. In fact, "snuck" is not really a word.

**Spore vs. spoor**. *Spoor* refers to animal droppings or the scent by which an animal is traced; a *spore* is a seed.

**Stanch vs. staunch**. *Staunch* means firm (a staunch supporter), while *stanch* means to stop the flow of something (money, blood).

**Stalk vs. stock**. To *stalk* means to hunt or harass; to *stock* means to add inventory (to stock a shelf, to stock a stream). *Stalking* means the act of hunting, but a pair of *stockings* (silk, nylon) is an undergarment worn by ladies.

**Standing room only.** Hyphenate before modified noun: a standing-room-only crowd; no hyphens if after the noun. The *AP Stylebook* disagrees, and also allows SRO, which I don't like because I don't feel the acronym is necessary.

**Stationary vs. stationery**. Distinguishing between these two words is a real problem for many people. *Stationary* is the act of remaining motionless, while *stationery* refers to writing paper.

**Straight-laced, strait-laced, strait-jacket**. *Straight-laced* refers to a morally conservative person, while *strait-laced* and *strait-jacket* refer to a restrictive, corset-type garment.

**Suit vs. suite**. A *suite* is used to describe music, furniture, rooms (of a hotel) and rhymes with sweet, while a *suit* refers to clothing or cards.

**Summary vs. summery**. A *summary* is a recapitulation of evidence, while *summery* means summer-like.

**Takeaway.** One word.

**Taught vs. taut**. *Taught* is the past tense of teach, and *taut* means something (cloth, skin) that is pulled tight.

**Team vs. teem**. *Teem* (usually coupled with *with*) means to be filled with, to abound (the stream was teeming with trout eager to take my fly), while a *team* is a group of people coming together for some common purpose, often —but not always—to participate in a sporting event. Note: *teamwork* is one word.

**Telephone numbers.** The preferred representation for telephone numbers in the United States is the three-digit area code in parentheses SPACE three-digit number HYPHEN four-digit number: (941) 706-2463. This is also acceptable: 941-706-2463.

**Temerity vs. timidity**. These words are almost opposite in nature: *temerity* means audacious, reckless, while *timidity* means to be timid, unsure.

**Tenant vs. tenet**. A *tenant* rents space from a landlord; a *tenet* is a fundamental principle or opinion.

**That vs. which**. Use *that* when introducing a restrictive clause that specifies a thing. (Which one? That one!)

Use *which* to refer to information that is not essential to the meaning of a sentence.

Example: The red dress, which was the tightest of them all, was the one that I chose to wear.

A comma often precedes *which;* a comma never precedes *that*.

**There vs. their**. I never thought I'd have to include this listing until I saw "their" used for "there" yesterday in a Huffington Post article. I emailed the writer (Subject line: "Huge typo in HuffPo article!"), who promptly and appreciatively wrote back, and—hopefully—made the necessary correction. That's a really bad mistake.

**Through, threw, thru**. This is easy: "thru" is not a real word—don't use it. *Through* means in at one end and out at the other, while *threw* is the past tense of the verb "throw."

**Till vs. 'til**. Both of these words are used as a contraction of "until." However, since *till* is also a verb ("I had to till the land") as well as a noun ("He cleaned out the till") some might argue that it's easier to use *'til* as a contraction for until, to avoid confusion. Still, the *King James Bible* and the 1928 *Book of Common Prayer* use till, and those are two weighty authorities.

**Timeframe, timeframes.** One word. I don't like it, but I don't always get my way.

**Torpid, torrid, turbid, turgid**. *Torpid* means sluggish, while *torrid* can mean the opposite: fast, furious, hot, passionate. Example: He set a torrid pace. *Turbid* means clouded, muddied, disturbed, and is usually used to describe liquid or gases. *Turgid* means to be swollen with liquid or gas.

**Torturous vs. tortuous**. The word *torturous* is related to torture, as in painful, while *tortuous* means full of twists and turns, circuitous.

**Toward, towards, untoward**. The definitions of *toward* and *towards* are identical. Some style guides note a rise in the use of towards because of its ease in conversational use. However, the *AP Stylebook* says that there is no "s" at the end of the word. The key thing is to be consistent throughout your work. If you use toward sometimes and towards other times, one version will be what we call a typo. *Untoward* ("untowards" is not correct) means unfortunate, improper (especially behavior).

**Trade off.** Two words as a verb; hyphenated as a noun and adjective.

**Tread.** The past tense of the verb tread is *trod,* unless you are using it in the "treading water" sense, and then, according to *The New York Times*, it is *treaded.*

**Trigger-happy.** Hyphenated.

**Turnout.** One word as a noun: The turnout at my Miami program was so good they had to unlock closets and drag out dusty chairs. Two words as a verb, though it is a rather awkward verb.

**TV.** An acceptable abbreviation for television. Capitalize.

**Undo vs. undue.** *Undo* means to go back a step, to unfasten, to untie. *Undue* means unnecessary, excessive, inappropriate.

**United States of America.** Abbreviate as U.S.A., with periods, only when used as an adjective. Spell out when used as a noun. Capitalize "states" when referring to the U.S.A.: I am from the States.

**Unkempt vs. unkept**. *Unkept* means unfulfilled, as in "His most important promise went unkept." *Unkempt* means not taken care of properly (hair, shrubbery, appearance in general).

**Unwanted vs. unwonted**. *Unwanted* means unwelcome, while *unwonted* means unusual, rare.

**On vs. upon.** These words are so similar that it's difficult to distinguish between them. However, you'd never say something like "I was upon time," so they can't be used entirely interchangeably.

**Use to vs. used to.** This is interesting! Use the phrase "used to" + verb in a positive sense: I *used to* be a jock. Use the phrase "use to" + verb when you refer to something negatively: I didn't *use to* be a jock.

**Vice vs. vise**. A *vice* (noun) is an evil or immoral habit; a *vise* (noun) is an instrument that holds two things together, or, when used as a verb, the act of holding, pressing, or squeezing. Also, it's *vice versa*, not vise versa or visa versa.

**Vicious vs. viscous.** I saw this in the description for a self-published book: the killer was *viscous*, which means having a sticky or thick consistency. I'd imagine the author meant that the killer was *vicious*, as in extraordinarily violent, inflicting harm on someone or something with deliberate malice.

**Way.** *Way* is not synonymous with *very*; unless you are 12, avoid that use.

**Weather, whether, wither, whither**. These are all real words, of course, and worthy of a quick check.

**Weave.** The verb *weave* has two meanings. The first meaning, an intransitive verb, pertains to thread, fabric, pattern; the past tense of this meaning is wove and woven. The second meaning, a transitive verb, is to dodge, to zigzag, to twist and turn—generally to avoid a barrier or obstructions; the past tense is weaved.

Examples:

The author had carefully woven the clues to the murderer's identity throughout the story.

We weaved our way through the bobbing boats to the dock.

**White paper.** Two words, no capitals.

**Who vs. whom**. This is really pretty simple: *who* is used as a subject, and *whom* is used as an object.

Subjects do the action: He/she/they/I/we walked the dog.

Objects receive the action:

The dog was walked by him/her/them/me/us.

Use *who* for subjects and *whom* for objects.

Examples:

Who walked the dog?

The dog was walked by whom?

This rule also applies to *whoever* and *whomever*: whoever is the subject; whomever is the object.

**Wi-Fi.** Two capital letters, hyphenated.

**Word-of-mouth.** Hyphenated as both a noun and adjective.

**Word processing.** As verb, no hyphen. As a noun, the accepted spelling is *word processor*, with the *-or.*

**World War I, World War II.** Do not abbreviate. Use World War I or World War II in all references.

**Wreath vs. wreathe.** A *wreath* (noun) is a circlet of flowers or vines, while to *wreathe* (verb) is the act of placing a wreath on something: The winner was wreathed with a wreath of roses.

## Part 2: Homonym list.

Many of the "Commonly Misused/Misspelled Words" are homonyms (which are also called homophones), but this is a list of homonyms that would be less likely to be confused with one another. (However, when I do see one of these word pairs misused, I tend to move the pair up into the previous section.)

If you know of a homonym that I've missed, please let me know.

Note: Spell check *will not* catch an improper use!

Acts/ax/axe, ad/add, adieu/ado, aid/aide, ail/ale, air/heir, airy/aerie, aisle/isle, all/awl, aloud/allowed, ant/aunt, arc/ark, assistance/assistants, ate/eight, auger/augur, aught/ought, aural/oral, away/aweigh, awed/odd, awful/offal, bald/balled/bawled, balm/bomb, band/banned, bar/barre, baron/barren, based/baste, be/bee, beach/beech, beat/beet, beau/bow, beaut/butte, been/bin, belle/bell, berg/burg, berry/bury, berth/birth, bier/buyer, billed/build, bite/bight/byte, blue/blew, boar/bore, board/bored, boarder/border, bolder/boulder, bole/bowl, borough/burrow, bough/bow, brake/break, breach/breech, bread/bred, brewed/brood, bridal/bridle, broach/brooch, brows/browse, brut/brute, burger/burgher, bus/buss, bussed/bust, but/butt, buy/by/bye, cache/cachet, cache/cash, caddy/catty, call/caul, caller/collar, canter/cantor, carol/carrel, cast/caste, caster/castor, caught/cot, cause/caws, cede/seed, ceiling/sealing, cell/sell, cellar/seller, censer/censor/sensor, cent/scent/sent, cents/sense/since, cereal/serial, chalk/chock, chary/cherry, chased/chaste, cheap/cheep, chews/choose, chili/chilly, chute/shoot, clause/claws, click/clique, climb/clime, close/clothes, coarse/course, colonel/kernel, conch/conk, coo/coup, core/corps, creak/creek, crews/cruise, cue/queue, currant/current, cygnet/signet, cymbal/symbol, dam/damn, daughter/dodder, dawn/don, days/daze, dear/deer, den/din, dhole/dole, disgust/discussed, do/dew/due, doe/dough, does/doze, drier/dryer, dual/duel, dun/done, dye/die, earn/urn, eave/eve, eek/eke, epic/epoch, ewe/yew/you, facts/fax, fain/feign, faint/feint, fair/fare, fairy/ferry, faux/foe, faun/fawn, feat/feet, file/phial, find/fined, fir/fur, fisher/fissure, flack/flak, flea/flee, flecks/flex, flocks/phlox, flew/flu/flue, floe/flow, flour/flower, for/fore/four, fort/forte, forth/fourth, foul/fowl, franc/frank, freeze/frieze, friar/fryer, gaff/gaffe, gaiter/gator, gamble/gambol, genes/jeans, gild/gilled/guild, gilt/guilt, gnawed/nod, gorilla/guerrilla, gram/graham, grate/great, grill/grille, grisly/grizzly, groan/grown, guarantee/guaranty, guessed/guest, guise/guys, hail/hale, hair/hare, handsome/hansom, hall/haul, hart/heart, hawk/hock, hay/hey, heal/heel, hear/here, hence/hints, herd/heard, heroin/heroine, hew/hue, hi/hie/high, higher/hire, him/hymn, hoar/whore, hoard/horde, hoarse/horse, hole/whole, holey/wholly/holy, hostel/hostile, hour/our, humerus/humorous, hurdle/hurtle, idle/idol/idyll, in/inn, incidence/incidents, jam/jamb, junkie/junky, knave/nave, knead/need, knew/new, knight/night, knit/nit, knob/nob, knot/naught/not, koi/coy, know/no, knows/nose, lacks/lax, ladder/latter, lam/lamb, lay/lei, lead/lede, leader/liter, leach/leech, leak/leek, lean/lien, leased/least, lends/lens, lent/lint, lesser/lessor, levee/levy, lichen/liken, lie/lye, links/lynx, lite/light, lo/low, load/lode, loan/lone, loch/lock, locks/lox, loop/loupe, loot/lute, mach/mock, maid/made, mail/male, main/mane/mein, maize/maze, mall/maul/moll, mantel/mantle, mark/marque, marry/merry, marquee/marquise, marshal/martial, massed/mast, mat/matte, me/mi, mean/mien, meant/mint, meat/meet/mete, medal/meddle, metal/mettle, mews/muse, mewl/mule, might/mite, miner/minor, mince/mints, mind/mined, missal/missile, missed/mist, moan/mown, moat/mote, mode/mowed, moiré/moray, moose/mousse, morn/mourn, morning/mourning, muscle/mussel, mussed/must, mustard/mustered, mutual/mutuel, nay/neigh, nicks/nix, none/nun, oar/o'er/or/ore, oh/owe, one/won, overdo/overdue, overseas/oversees, paced/paste, packed/pact, pail/pale, pain/pane, pair/pare/pear, parish/perish, patience/patients, pause/paws, peace/piece, peak/peek/pique, peal/peel, pearl/purl, pedal/peddle/petal, peer/pier, pennants/penance, per/purr, pin/pen, pistil/pistol, place/plaice, plain/plane, plait/plate, pleas/please, plough/plow, plum/plumb, pocks/pox, pole/poll, pomace/pumice, praise/prays/preys, premier/premiere, presence/presents, prince/prints, prise/prize, psi/sigh, profit/prophet, purest/purist, quarts/quartz, quince/quints, rack/wrack, rail/rale, rap/wrap, rapt/wrapped, ray/re, real/reel, read/red, read/reed, reek/wreak, residence/residents, rest/wrest, retch/wretch, review/revue, rheum/room, right/rite/write, ring/wring, road/rode/rowed, roe/row, roil/royal, role/roll, root/route, rose/rows, rot/wrought, rote/wrote, rough/ruff, rude/rued, rung/wrung, rye/wry, sachet/sashay, sale/sail, sane/seine, sawed/sod, scull/skull, sea/see, seas/sees/seize, seam/seem, seamen/semen, sects/sex, seen/scene, seraph/serif, serf/surf, shake/sheik, shoe/shoo, shone/shown, sign/sine, sic/sick, side/sighed, sighs/size, sink/sync/synch, slay/sleigh, sleight/slight, slew/slough, slough/slow, soar/sore, soared/sword, some/sum, son/sun, sole/soul, sonny/sunny, sot/sought, spade/spayed, spec/speck, staff/staph, stake/steak, staid/stayed, statice/status, straight/strait, stare/stair, steal/steel, step/steppe, stile/style, stolen/stollen, sty/stye, succor/sucker, suede/swayed, suite/sweet, sundae/Sunday, tach/tack, tacked/tact, tacks/tax, tail/tale, tare/tear, taught/taut, tea/tee, tear/tier, ten/tin, tender/tinder, tense/tents, tent/tint, tern/turn, the/thee, their/there, threw/through, throes/throws, throne/thrown, thyme/time, tic/tick, tide/tied, tighten/titan, toad/toed/towed, to/too/two, toe/tow, told/tolled, tongue/tung, tort/torte, tray/trey, troop/troupe, trussed/trust, vain/vane/vein, vale/veil, vary/very, vial/vile, vice/vise, waddle/wattle, wade/weighed, wail/wale/whale, wain/wane, waist/waste, wait/weight, waive/wave, wales/whales, walk/wok, want/wont, ware/wear/where, way/weigh/whey, we/wee, weak/week, weal/wheel, weather/whether, wench/winch, wet/whet, which/witch, whig/wig, while/wile, whine/wine, whirled/world, whit/wit, whither/wither, whoa/woe, wood/would, word/whirred, world/whirled, worst/wurst, yay/yeah, yew/you, yoke/yolk

**British and French spellings.**

The spelling differences between British and American English are legion, a minefield, really, numbering in the thousands. American English words ending in -or, -ize, -ization, -er, -y, and -g should be double-checked. These common words are identical in meaning, but not in spelling; American English is the first word, and that (for American writers) is the preferred use.

Aluminum/aluminium, armor/armour, behavior/behaviour, caché/cachet, cancelation/cancellation, capitalize/capitalise, catalog/catalogue, categorize/categorise, center/centre, check/cheque, color/colour, curb/kerb, dialog/dialogue, donut/doughnut, emphasize/emphasise, energize/energise, favor/favour, fiber/fibre, flavor/flavour, glamor/glamour, gray/grey, harbor/harbour, honor/honour, inquiry/enquiry, jail/gaol, jewelry/jewellery, labor/labour, maneuver/manoeuvre, math/maths, meter/metre, minimize/minimise, neighbor/neighbour, organize/organise, organization/organisation, parlor/parlour, personalize/personalise, program/programme, publicize/publicise, realize/realise, recognize/recognise, rigor/rigour, savor/savour, shop/shoppe, skeptical/sceptical, specialize/specialise, standardize/standardise, story/storey, summarize/summarise, theater/theatre, tire/tyre, ton/tonne, traveler/traveller, tumor/tumour, veranda/verandah, vigor/vigour, whiskey/whisky

**And, just because there's room...**

Here's a list of words that are spelled the same but have different meanings, depending on their pronunciation. It seems as though the words that are noun/verbs are accented on the first syllable when a noun, but the second syllable when a verb. Interesting. This list is especially important for poets; in other words, you might want to use *another* word if you are thinking about one of these.

Abuse, address, advocate, aggregate, alternate, appropriate, articulate, attribute, August/august, bass, bow, buffet, close, closer, collect, combine, commiserate, commune, complex, compress, conduct, confine, console, consummate, content, contest, convert, curate, decline, defect, delegate, deliberate, desert, detail, digest, discount, dispatch, does, dove, elaborate, empire, entrance, envelope, evening, excuse, gallant, graduate, homage, house, intimate, intrigue, invalid, lead, live, minute, misuse, mobile, moderate, object, offense, outfit, patent, perfect, Polish/polish, present, produce, progress, project, putting, rebel, record, recreate, refuse, resign, retard, separate, slough, sow, subject, suspect, tear, trusty, upset, use, wind, wound

## Foreign words and phrases that everyone should know.

An asterisk precedes words or phrases that don't need to be italicized. Also, unless noted, none of these words or phrases are proper nouns, so no capitalization is necessary.

***A cappela** (ah ka PEL lah)—voices without instrumental accompaniment

**À demain** (Ah DUH meh)—a synonym for goodbye that literally means "on the morrow."

**A priori** (Ah pray OR ay)—deductively

**Ad hoc** (ad hock)—created for a specific purpose

***Art nouveau** (are noo VOH)—style of the late 19th and early 20th centuries, characterized by curving forms and motifs based on nature, e.g., leaves, vines, flowers.

**À propos** (a pro POH)—appropriate, in relation to ("À propos of nothing in particular…"). Also correct as one word or hyphenated: apropos and à-propos; the accent is optional.

**Au courant** (oh coo rah)—with it, of the moment (in a good way—opposite would be passé, which means out of date)

***Bauhaus** (bow [as in bow wow] house)—1910s—1930s movement characterized by mass-production, simplified functionality. Note: this is a proper noun and is always capitalized.

***Beaux arts** (boh zar)—literally, fine art

***Blitzkrieg** (blitz kreeg)—literally, lightning war; a swift and overwhelming attack

**Cadeau** (cad OH)—a gift

**Carte blanche** (cart blansh)—a blank check; freedom to do…whatever

**Caveat** (cav EE aht)—a warning

**Chiaroscuro** (key ah roh SKEW row)—the distribution of light versus shade in a picture

**Cognoscenti** (CONYOH shenti) a connoisseur

**Comme il faut** (come eel foh)—proper, as it should be

***Connoisseur** (CONO sir) an appreciative expert

**Coup de grâce** (KOO duh GRAH)—a death blow

**De rigueur** (duh rih GRR)—required by the standards of the day

**Deus ex machina** (DAY us ex MAH key nah)—literally, "God in a machine"; a theatrical device whereby the solution to a problem arrives out of the blue.

**Dolce vita** (dole cha vee ta)—life of ease

**Double entendre** (double on ton drah)—a word or phrase with two meanings, one of which is usually risqué.

**Exegesis** (ex ah GEE sis)—a critical interpretation, examination, or exploration of writing, especially of religious texts like the Bible.

**Faux pas** (foh pah)—a social misstep

***Götterdämmerung** (got er dahm er oong)—dusk (ending) of the Gods. A proper noun, and so is always capitalized.

**Hoi polloi** (hoy puh loy)—common people, the masses

**Homage** (oh MAJ) is a noun, typically used to indicate an art form (painting, film, etc.) that was created to honor another artist's style or technique (an homage to Picasso, an homage to Alfred Hitchcock). Homage (HAH madge), also a noun, means to offer recognition or honor in a substantive way, and is usually part of the phrase *pay homage to* such-and-such: The statue paid homage to the town's founder.

**Hors de combat** (ore duh com bah)—out of action due to an injury

***Hors d'oeuvres** (ore derves)—appetizers

***Hubris** (HEW bris)—excessive pride. Note: Two syllables, not three.

**Ignominy.** *Ignominy* means public shame or embarrassment, and it's pronounced **ig'** nah min ee.

**In camera** (just like it looks)—private, usually a conference in a judge's chambers

**In lieu** (in loo)—in place of

**In loco parentis** (just like it looks)—in place of parent

**In situ** (just like it looks)—undisturbed, in its original place

**In toto** (just like it looks)—in total, as a whole

**Je ne sais quoi** (jeh nuh say kwa)—a certain undefinable something

**Joie de vivre** (jzwha duh veevra)—joy in life. Sorry about the "j" sound; it's a French thing.

**Obiter dictum** (OB it er dic TUM)—a remark made in passing

**Objet d'art** (OBE jhzay dar)—small objects of artistic value: a collection of hand blown glass paperweights would be a good example

**Le mot juste** (leh moh jhzoost)—the right word in the right place

**Louche** (loosh)—morally dubious

**Magnum opus** (magnum OH pus)—the most important work by an artist

**Mater** (MATE er) Latin for mother

**Mea culpa** (mee ah COOL pah)—through my fault

**Milieu** (mill YEH)—environment

**Modus operandi** (MODE is op er en dye)—the way someone or something operates. Plural: modi operendi.

Modus vevendi (MODUS viv en dye)--a way of life, a manner of living, a feasible arrangement

**Naïf** (nah EEF)—a naive person (pronounced just like naive but with an *eeff* sound at the end).

**Ne plus ultra** (ne plooz ultra)—nothing higher or better

**Noblesse oblige** (NO bless oh BLEEJHZ)—the obligation of the nobility and/or well educated to act better than the masses

**Nom de plume** (just like it looks)—pen name

**Nonpareil** (non par EL)—don't be surprised if you see this word as two (non pareil), especially in older texts. It means peerless.

**Non sequitur** (non seck quit er)—an illogical conclusion

**Nouveau riche** (NOO voh reesh)—newly rich

**Pater** (PAW ter) Latin for father

***Pelagic** (pell AH jick)—pertaining to the open ocean.

**Persona non grata** (per SOHNA non grat a)—an unwelcome person

**Piano nobile** (piano NOH bee lay)—ground floor of a large home

**Pièce de résistance** (P S duh RAY sis tahnse)—something outstanding; the thing you can't resist

**Pied-à-terre** (pee ed ah tair)—a small apartment for visits of short duration

***Plethora** (PLETH rah)—many. Note: two syllables, not three.

**Quid pro quo** (just like it looks)—tit for tat

**Quixotic** (kwix OT ick)—a mission with little chance of success

**Raconteur** (rah con TER)—a skilled storyteller; this is the male version of this word; the feminine version is raconteuse (rah con TUHZ)

**Raison d'etre** (RAY zon det reh)—reason for being

**Roman-à-clef** (ROW ma nah cleh)—a novel in which real people and/or events are represented using fictitious names

**Sang-froid** (sahn frwah)—literally, cold blood; self-possession, bravery in the face of danger

**Schadenfreude** (sha den froid eh)—a delight in another's misfortune

**Sine qua non** (sin ee qua non)—a given, an indispensable element

**Sobriquet** (sew bri KAY)—a nickname, sometimes humorous or unflattering

**Soi-disant** (swa DEE zahn)—self-styled

**Sotto voce** (SAH toe VOH chee)—to say something under your breath, at half volume (which is not the same as a whisper)

**Sturm und drang** (sturm und drahng)—drama, tension, upheaval

**Sub rosa** (just like it looks)—privately

**Sui generis** (SO ee GEN er us) in a class by itself

**Summa cum laude** (SUE ma koom LOUD ay)—with highest praise; there is also cum laude and magna cum laude; these are used to designate college degrees with special honors.

**Tabula rasa** (TAB you la RAS a)—a mind undisturbed by experiences, a blank slate

**Terra incognita** (TAIR ah in cog NEE ta)—uncharted territory

**Tête-à-tête** (tet ah tet)—a private conversation between two people.

**Tout de suite** (toot sweet)—with haste

***Verboten** (ver BOH ten)—forbidden

***Voilà** (VWA lah)—An interjection that is difficult to translate, but “Here it is!” or “Here you are!” is pretty close. I’d suggest that the “a” get that accent.

**Volte-face** (volt fahss)—complete change of position or opinion.

***Zeitgeist** (zite guyst)—the spirit of the time

## Chapter 3: Writing.

**Rule #1. Don't be trendy.**

**Rule #2. Watch for repetitive words, phrases, and sentence structure.**

**Rule #3. Continuity.**

**Before you PRINT or PUBLISH.**

### Rule #1. Don't be trendy.

I mentioned the issue of clichés at the very beginning of this book, and I included a list of words (right off the top of my head, for the most part) that I believe are rocketing toward trite status, if they haven't already arrived. When I read someone's writing that includes three or more of those words or phrases, I don't think thought *leader*; no, I think *follower*.

I'm not saying that you should never use any of those words or phrases (though the next time someone refers to me as a *guy*, I'm going to go nuts), but guard against overuse. When people see the same vocabulary over and over again, those words become stale. Those words become stale quick. In fact, the shelf life of words has never been shorter.

Take a look at these sentences:

On these special occasions when my sore throat was deemed risky enough that I scored a day on the couch in my PJs, I turned to one author and one author only: C.S. Lewis.

Shoot to write 1-2 blogs per week and gradually increase from there.

You guys can implement this with your brand and your office.

Training was awesome and really got me going.

To help you identify what's effective and what's not, I've listed out the following 17 examples of CTAs that totally rock.

"Totally rock"? "Awesome"? "Shoot to"? *Nooooooo!*

Those sentences in the previous example are a little too young, a little too immature, to be considered good writing. Nor will those words, in my opinion, stand the test of time.

And watch your language! Strive to be friendly and accessible, but not stupid. If you are an educated person, sound like it.

Example: Most small trade publishers like us suck at social.

Unless you are working on fiction or memoir, words like *suck* have no place in college-level and business writing. Period. Ditto almost all words referring to bodily functions, *blink, chew,* and *swallow* excepted. No shitting, no fucking, no puking. No pissing. Winking? Okay. Peeing? No way! No, no, and **NO**. You don't have to sound prissy, but you do need to sound *professional.*

### Rule #2. Watch for repetitive words, phrases, and sentence structure.

Sure, you are building a style. You are developing a body of work. And, of course, you have your own voice. That's great.

What's not great, however, is to lean on certain words, phrases, and sentence structure that will have your professors snoozing. *Repetitive* is almost as bad as *trendy.*

For example, the co-founder of a major internet-based business, an MIT grad who's obviously no slouch, wrote a book a couple of years back. In this book, he used humorous parenthetical asides with some regularity. How regular is regular, you ask? How about 57 times. And it's not that long of a book! What was fun and endearing at the beginning became annoying.

Believe me, his reliance on that structure got old in a hurry, and yet it went on and on and on.

Frankly, that's the kind of thing his editor should have caught. The majority of writers out there don't have an editor. We have to do these things ourselves. (That's where the *self* in *Self-Editing for the Successful Pre-Law Student* comes in!)

Many of us have favorite go-to words and phrases. That's okay. I myself am partial to *schadenfreude, raison d'etre*, and *in loco parentis. Cognoscenti*? It's a personal favorite! What can I say? Well, I *can* say that I don't use those words often, especially in my writing. Always remember: the more unusual the word or phrase, the fewer times it can be used in each piece your write. The clock resets with the start of every essay, story, blog, article, and paper, but within those entities you've got to be aware of your use of words.

A separate but definitely related issue is sentence structure. Make sure that you vary your sentence structure. For example, I recently had a client who used a "not only this, but this, this, and this" sentence structure five times in a very brief article. It was noticeable. Another thing to think about is this: avoid beginning your sentences the same way, i.e., with the same word or phrase. Take a look at this biographical piece:

> Until January, 2012, she was the Director of the Institute for Public Policy and Leadership at the University of South Florida Sarasota-Manatee campus, in Sarasota, Florida. She left USF to form her own Consulting Company focused on Resiliency based in Innate Health. She also serves as an Initiative Consultant for The Patterson Foundation of Sarasota, Florida, on a collaborative project to transform the curriculum at the Ringling College of Art and Design. She is the Chairman of the Board for Realize Bradenton, and is a member of the Board of the Manatee Healthcare Alliance. She is President of Manatee Tiger Bay, an organization for the discussion and debate of public policy. She is on the board of several other civic organizations. She serves as a consultant and trainer in Innate Health for other organizations and practitioners globally, including the creation of an Innate Health curriculum for a college in South Africa.

Basically, seven sentences start with "she." The four previous, unquoted, sentences started with "she." In the final paragraph, "she" or "her" are the only references to "her"—her name appears only one time in three paragraphs.

There are also other issues with the editing of this information, improper capitalization being just one, but the habit of starting so many sentences the same way is a real bore.

Before we continue, however, it is important to qualify the "no repetition" rule. The "no repetition" rule does not apply to deliberate rhetorical or stylistic devices, which can be used very effectively from time to time. A famous example of repetition, which is properly called "parallel construction" (when it's done in a good way), is found in Winston Churchill's famous "Speech on Dunkirk," delivered in the House of Commons. Once you've heard it, who can forget it? Who can fail to be stirred?

> ...[W]e shall fight on the beaches, we shall fight on the landing grounds, we shall fight in the fields and in the streets, we shall fight in the hills; we shall never surrender...

No, that's not the type of repetition I'm talking about; I'm talking about falling into a lazy, comfortable pattern of redundancy, boring your readers to death.

## Rule #3. Continuity.

Just about every question or problem you could have in your writing is discussed in this book. Use this book! Rarely am I faced with an issue that I can't look up here. I am, however, going to say a few words about one issue that hasn't really come up, and that's *continuity*.

In a movie scene, the actors often have to take breaks. Movie studios have a person whose job it is to make sure that things pick up *exactly* where they left off: the curtain rod is still down, the clock still says quarter-past, it is still raining, the lighting is just so. Things have to stay the same. Your ability to maintain consistent creative *and* editorial continuity is critical. Nothing will brand your work less than professional faster—aside from misspellings, missing words, punctuation and grammar mistakes—than lack of continuity within your writing.

**"Continuity" may mean a number of things.**

If you are going to establish a method of showing the English translation of foreign words, for example, and you need to use the method many times in your writing, be consistent. If you are going to show the correct pronunciation of a word next to the written word, the *AP Stylebook* suggests putting the pronunciation in parentheses immediately after the name, with the accented syllable in caps and followed by an apostrophe, and you need to follow this method every time. (FYI: This works well with written text; however, when you are writing an introduction that will be read by someone else, I'd suggest putting the accented syllable in BOLD, for easier reading.)

Similarly, you must display all weights, measurements, heights, distances, money, and so on in the same way throughout your content. If you are writing for an American audience, use American measurements and spellings; the one exception would be if you are writing about your travels in a foreign country.

If you write a bullet point list, be sure the points are consistent; in other words, don't have some full-sentence points interspersed with points that consist of phrases.

For example, if some of your writing says that the name of your school is *The XYZ*, with a capital T in *The*, then you can't say *the XYZ* later. If you write a place name and that place name needs hyphens, make sure that each and every mention of that place includes the hyphens. Similarly, if you use a hyphenated version of a word (non-fiction) in one place, don't use the unhyphenated version (nonfiction) in another. (By the way: it's *nonfiction*—one word.)

Here is a good example of non-continuity (which is really not a word but is appropriate just the same). These are two sentences in two different job listings from an internet business's "Jobs" page:

We are looking for a Director of Sales Development to build out, manage, and execute a world class business development program.

Can you lead teams of designers, producers and artists to create world-class marketing campaigns?

You can say world-class or world class, but not both (and, in both these cases, world-class with the hyphen was correct).

If you use a word (windowsill) in one place, don't write it as two words (window sill) in another. Ditto sawmill, dining room, courthouse, darkroom, and so on. The time you spend confirming that "ringmaster" and "fistfight" and "headdresses" are, in fact, *one* word is time well spent. Your professor will appreciate it if you attach a note saying something like, "I looked this up. It *is* one word," to the content. If you have an unusual or specialized vocabulary or if there are words that you are going to deliberately misspell ("feller" or "fella" for "fellow," for instance), make sure you let your professor know.

Double-check the names of the people you mention because no one forgets having his or her name misspelled. That person might laugh and say it was no big deal—don't believe it.

If you aren't completely, utterly, absolutely sure about something, for Pete's sake, look it up!

Page after page, essay after essay, term paper after term paper, chart and graphic after chart and graphic, paper to ebook—everything has to be the same. Continuity is the hallmark of a professional.

This sort of spade work is the responsibility of the *writer*. And don't think people won't notice. Trust me: they will.

## Before you PRINT or PUBLISH

Just before you print or publish, here is what to do.

The first thing is to put your content into Microsoft Word. Word can and will pick up lots of little mistakes. Turn on your Pilcrow (the ¶ sign) so that you can see all the spaces (which are represented as dots between words and symbols). Make sure there are no places where you've got two spaces after periods and colons; older writers who used to use that style will put two spaces after periods and colons without even thinking about it. Word will also pick up repeated words (deadly, and so difficult to see!), misspelled words that are out-and-out misspelled, and sometimes it will pick up noun-verb-pronoun confusion, missing apostrophes, and so on.

When I edit writing with words that aren't in my in-program dictionary, I always add the first use to the dictionary because that way any other time that unusual word is misspelled, I will see it. This is especially helpful in a work with a lot of foreign words.

Word is not infallible. Not at all. Word will not pick up on homonyms, for example. But, all in all, Word is helpful, so use it.

**The self-editing checklist.**

When you edit, you have to become another person; you have to wear a different hat. As an writer, you rush headlong, pell-mell, down a wordy path, because of your burning need to get your thrilling thoughts in black and white. Editing your own words is, however, an entirely different matter. Editing takes time. If perfection is your goal, then editing is the wide, tree-lined avenue filled with interesting sights, leading to perfect content. Never forget (even you atheists among us): God is in the details, not the devil. The devil is that impatient little voice inside your head that reminds you that you're pushing your deadline; the bossy little voice telling you that you are brilliant; you've done enough; you do not need to double-check your work. The devil will be perfectly happy if you turn in error-ridden content and look like a fool.

Fight the devil! Take your time! Make it perfect!

1. Watch for repetitive words and phrases. If you find a word or phrase you've used twice, chances are good that you've used it more than two times. On the second use, go back to your word processor and do a "search" for that word or phrase. "Bold" each example. Then go back to your reading, knowing that you've found things that will eventually need to be addressed as you move ahead.

2. Look for repetitive sentence structure. Once you've found a second example of repeated sentence structure, start to "bold" the element of repetition (the "as" sentence, the "but" sentence, sentences using the passive voice, and so on) so you can track your usage. When you edit, examine your usage, and, if you really lean on a particular sentence structure, try to vary it up a bit.

Note: A related issue to items 1 and 2 is repetitive *style*. Use italics and parenthetical asides with a light hand.

3. As you read, listen for inadvertent humor: does something rhyme when it shouldn't? Take a look at this sentence:

"This means that we don't just roll out a tool to drive sales, we can constantly work to increase yield and improve results," claims James.

"Claims James" might not be hysterically funny, but it is funny enough that another option should be considered.

4. Double-check your punctuation and look carefully at commonly misspelled words. Drag your eyes slowly over "it's" and "its." I do a search for every use and it has saved my backside often.

Question *everything*. Is "every day" in the use you plan one word or two? Do you really remember that speech in *Romeo and Juliet* or the first stanza of that hymn? When in doubt, look it up, whether it is a word, a quote, a company name, or whatever.

5. Keep at it. Be stubborn. Check and double-check.

**Last-minute thoughts.**

Typos and misspelled words are all over the place. I've found typos and misspelled words in fine nonfiction, like Isabel Wilkerson's *The Warmth of Other Suns*, which won the Pulitzer Prize, as well as popular fiction like *The Hunger Games*, by Suzanne Collins. Both of these authors had top-notch editors and support staff, I'm sure. So, so what? It happens. I just do my best to make sure that it doesn't happen to *me*.

As you are finalizing your work, do a search for double spaces. Go to your search box and hit space, space; even though nothing will show in the box, the spaces are there and will be found by the search function. You might be surprised how many slip through. Double-check that all letters and symbols in an italicized word or phrase are actually *in* italics. Repeated punctuation marks like parentheses, commas, and periods are also very difficult to catch. I have a list of words that I'm notorious for misspelling (*were* and *where* come immediately to mind), so I do a search for all those words. Search for duplicated "small" words: if *if*, and *and*, the *the*, of *of*, a *a* (this'll drive you crazy, but do it anyway), so *so*, and so on.

**The bottom line.** There are no "little" mistakes. The top students are perfect. Perfection = good grades. Perfection is achievable: pull out all the stops to make your writing perfect.

## Last test!

Time for a full-on edit. Everything is up for grabs.

Let's see what you've learned. Answers follow.

1. This is quoted material from a blog post.

Apple has a huge number of people that spread their love for the products they make. Buffer is engrossing a community of startup transparency thanks to some of their latest initiatives like the open metrics dashboard powered by Baremetrics or their open salaries posts. Ryan and the team at Product Hunt really care about the power of a 'true engaged community', and 'not just acquire additional users'. At the end, it seems 'easy' to grow a community if what you do is good enough.

2. From an interview in T*he New York Times*:

"New downtown merchants are like, 'Chief, I can't have customers outside,'" said the Daytona Beach police chief, Mike Chitwood. "They are panhandling, urinating and sleeping in my doorway because they know someone is coming to feed them."

3. A blog post reply credited to a website developing company.

Many times we have seen that due to complexity or even other problem like delay in page lode or so many steps in forum feeling to buy a products frustrate a user.

4. From a website.

It usually makes it easier for designers to synthesize the information they're given from the onset, too, instead of making changes along the way.

5. From a blog post.

For the designer, then, the initial meeting is all about gathering the necessary information -- such as the intended audience, problems that need to be addressed, and general tonal direction -- so they can then determine the concept, project scope, deliverables, and deadlines.

6. From website content.

If you are framing a long message or an essay, consider additional factors. A well-framed longer message includes:

- A title or headline that tells the reader what the message is about and why they should care.
- No more than one key message.
- A lead paragraph that captures the reader's attention.
- A "nut" paragraph (i.e. the heart of your story — the details go here).
- Relevant quotes to make the topic more relatable.

7. More website content.

Their feedback will at least give you insight into potential confusion or misunderstanding of the terminology in your messages.

8. From a blog post.

Joining a company with a culture and personality that align with your values and that support your ambitions will ultimately make you happier and more successful in your new position.

9. From an internet article.

The old adage that comes to mind is "Give a man a fish, he'll eat for a day, teach a man how to fish and he'll eat for a lifetime".

10. From website content.

My good friend and me will be co-hosting a two-part webinar series this month.

11. From website content.

He runs Product Strategy and Corporate Development at XYZ, a software company based in Cambridge, MA. At XYZ Brian is responsibile for strategic planning, pricing & packaging and corporate development. Additionally, Brian focuses on the design of XYZ's business processes and operational metrics.

Prior to joining XYZ Brian was a consultant concentrating on operational innovation at PRM.

Brian holds an MBA from MIT Sloan where he is an occassional guest lecturer as part of the new enterprises curriculum. He also holds a B.A. in Computer Science from Amherst College.

12. From website content.

Along with understanding the steps necessary to develop an effective estate plan, our talented advocates mediate and litigate disputes that arise during administration of a trust or estate.

13. More website content.

Julie combines an open and welcoming personality, contagious sense of humor and astute head for business that has propelled her to be consistently approached as an expert in personal and business branding and being the "CEO of YOU".

14. As oftentimes there is a lot of ambiguity innate in the law and the written words of a contract, a lawyer can facilitate that your legal rights are enforced.

15. From *Florida Small Claims Rules Annotated* (2020-2021 edition):

A party in a small claims case may file a motion for attorney's fees, even if represented by counsel, notwithstanding the general rule that a motion filed a party represented by counsel is considered a nullity.

## Answers.

1. Where to start? This writing has a little something for everyone!

A company is singular. A company is an *it*.

We've got pronoun confusion: "their" love refers to "people," but "they make" refers to Apple's products.

I'm not convinced that e*ngrossing*, which means to acquire, to absorb, to engage, is a good choice here. Plus, there's the word "gross" in engross, which has a negative connotation. But, let's try it, using several of its synonyms.

Buffer is *acquiring* a community of startup transparency...

Buffer is *absorbing* a community of startup transparency...

Buffer is *engaging* a community of startup transparency...

Well, I was confused. I thought it must be because I didn't "get" what a "startup transparency" was, so I went to Buffer.com to check it out. Ooops, wrong website. Further reading indicated that I should go to Bufferopen.com. Ooops, wrong website.

Is it me, or shouldn't the author of this paragraph have given me the tools to find "Buffer," or am I the only person on the planet who doesn't know what Buffer is?

After much searching, I found Buffer at Bufferapp.com.

I looked around and came away quickly, not much wiser for the experience.

I don't like engrossing. It's wrong. I think the author meant *embracing*. Embracing works, it fits, and it's a lot more positive a word.

And why use the conjunctive "or" here? Buffer is embracing "startup transparency" thanks to two things, so you'd want to use "and," not "or."

I found Product Hunt immediately. However, the single quotes are flat-out incorrect, and doubly incorrect when placed inside the comma and period. Plus, there seems to be a missing word in the phrase "not just acquire additional users."

And what's with the quotes around "easy"? Forget (for a moment) that those are single quotes and not double quotes; what I want to know is why are the quotes there in the first place?

Chapter 3: Writing.

I do think the tag line "...if what you do is good enough" is kind of funny, in a sad kind of way, given the fact that this writing isn't good enough. Not at all.

The funniest thing is that the blogger was so impressed with this lousy writing that he quoted it. He didn't write it, he quoted it. I'm amazed.

Here's a much better version:

Apple has a huge number of people who spread their love for the products Apple makes. Bufferapp.com is embracing startup transparency, thanks to its latest initiatives, including its open salaries posts and Baremetrics-powered open metrics dashboard. Ryan and the team at ProductHunt.com really care about the power of a "true engaged community." At the end of the day, it seems easy to grow a community if what you do is remarkable.

Certainly one of the takeaways is to include the correct name of all websites you reference, if any of those websites aren't exactly household names.

2. This is kind of tough, but it looks as if the chief continues to quote from the downtown merchants, but the single quotes to indicate that aren't there. Still, it's plain from the context that *he* isn't speaking (the "my doorway" hearkens back to the merchants), so I think—I *think*—that the writer just left out the second set of quotation marks that would indicate the quoting of a quote:

"New downtown merchants are like, 'Chief, I can't have customers outside,'" said the Daytona Beach police chief, Mike Chitwood. "'They are panhandling, urinating and sleeping in my doorway because they know someone is coming to feed them.'"

For a writer who made sure to quote the chief exactly, warts (the "like") and all, this is not careful reporting.

The takeaway here is to never, ever, let yourself be quoted saying "like" like that. That is, if you want to be, like, taken seriously.

I didn't capitalize or italicize the *T* in *The New York Times*. Did you catch it?

3. This post is so very sloppy. I know you're saying that it's just a post, but the person posting this reply gave his or her company's name, so it's not exactly anonymous.

There are a minimum of six misspelled/wrong words in this one sentence; it's such a mess that it's barely decipherable. Here's a stab at translation:

Many times we have seen that due to complexity or even other problems like delay in page load or too many steps in forum feeling [I'm lost here] to buy products frustrates a user.

Well, whatever. I wouldn't buy anything from that company!

4. It's *outset*, not *onset.*

It usually makes it easier for designers to synthesize the information they're given from the outset, too, instead of making changes along the way.

5. There are two problems with this sentence. First off, those are two hyphens (with spaces on both sides!) instead of the needed dashes.

Secondly, there's a noun-pronoun problem with the singular *the designer* and the plural *they.*

6. There are a number of problems with this bullet point list:

- Never put a colon after *including.* If you do want to introduce your points with a colon, say "including the following"
- Noun-pronoun mistake with "the reader" and "they"
- Comma missing after i.e.
- I am not keen on the use of "relatable." It is a very iffy word. Besides, relevant *is* relatable.

Because it's a style issue, the spaces between the dash and surrounding material are okay if the writer has been consistent (he was).

The bullet point list should look like this:

If you are framing a long message or an essay, consider additional factors. A well-framed longer message includes the following:

- A title or headline that tells readers what the message is about and why they should care.
- No more than one key message.
- A lead paragraph that captures the reader's attention.
- A "nut" paragraph (i.e., the heart of your story — the details go here).
- Quotes relevant to your readers.

7. Here's the "'or' equivalency" rearing its ugly head. Don't "confusion" and "misunderstanding" mean pretty much the same thing? Aren't they close enough that one can be dumped? I think so. This is better:

Their feedback will give you insight into potential problem areas in your message.

8. The subject of this sentence is *company*, which you can better see by trimming away the excess: A company that aligns with you and supports you will make you happier. So, both the verbs are incorrect.

Joining a company with a culture and personality that aligns with your values and that supports your ambitions will ultimately make you happier and more successful in your new position.

(I ignored *aligns*, which I dislike.)

9. We are missing a couple of punctuation marks in this give-a-man-a-fish saying that can't be ignored. First off, the way it's written, it's a comma splice. Secondly, we need a comma in the second section. Finally, quotation marks go *outside* periods and commas. There. Are. No. Exceptions. This sentence should have been written:

The old adage that comes to mind is "Give a man a fish, he'll eat for a day; teach a man how to fish, and he'll eat for a lifetime."

10. This sentence originally included names and company positions, so I took them out. The purpose of this entire exercise is to educate, not embarrass. Still, this is pretty awful. Take out the rest of the material and focus on the "me"—"me will be co-hosting"? Ugly, very ugly. The sentence should read:

My good friend and I will be co-hosting a two-part webinar series this month.

11. There are two misspelled words in this bio. It's inexcusable. The phrase "two misspellings" should never be in a sentence with the word "Amherst." That's not all that's wrong with this writing, but it's enough.

12. During [the] administration of a trust or estate.

13. No one who writes this kind of thing can possibly be taken seriously. I looked at this sentence for a long time and gave up. It needs a thorough rewrite, and I've, well, I've moved on. It's spam, pure and simple.

14. Ugh. Please don't ever write a sentence like this! Larded with unnecessary words though it is, the worst part of this sentence is "facilitate." It's absolutely the wrong word. Correct words could be "ensure" or even "guarantee," but never "facilitate."

15. Ooops! Find the missing word!

****

The thing about editing is that you improve with practice. Like any other skill, you get better the more you do it. You master the rules. You get more confident. Problematic material just leaps off the page. You learn and grow. This is fun stuff!

At EditNATION.com, I publish an editing quiz a couple of times a month, with the answers to the previous test published then, too. Practice, practice, practice.

Have you been editing *me*? I hope so! What adverb have I used 10 times in this text that also means "attractive"?

Get in the habit of editing *everyone*.

## Conclusion.

Believe it or not, *how* you write something is just about as important as *what* you write. Like it or not, how you package your message is just about as important as what that message is. Packaging means caring, packaging means attention to detail. Properly edited content is like the wrapping and bow on a gift; it's like the icing on the cake. In your mind's eye, imagine someone handing you an unwrapped gift or a birthday cake without the icing...aren't you just a little let down? You say to yourself: *It must have been a rush job.* Or: *He or she didn't care enough to make it special.* Aren't you just a teeny, tiny bit more excited when that extra effort has been made to wrap the gift or ice the cake? Just like cake by itself is pretty good, and an unwrapped gift is still a gift, aren't both the cake and the gift enhanced by their packaging? Oh, yes!

Attention to detail is the hallmark of *quality*.

Well, it's the same thing with your written words.

And the thing about it is this: people notice. People *recognize* quality. People *admire* quality. People *aspire* to quality. People *appreciate* quality. Especially the important people, like your friends, like your professors, like your potential boss.

Life is all about competition, even as you collaborate. Dotting your I's and crossing your T's will set you apart and give you a competitive edge over people who are just as smart, if not smarter. Being the go-to editing person in your class, in your dorm, at your job will make people sit up and take notice.

But even if no one seems to notice, does it really matter? *You* know. *You* are your most important audience. Trust me: Your ability to use vivid language to write remarkable content that's correctly expressed is a skill that will propel your life forward—influencing the people you know and people you'll never even meet. This is called leadership. Your mastery of punctuation and grammar rules will be noticeable and it will be valuable. Just watch and see.

In the meantime, *read.* Seth Godin manages to blog every day, and he knows his punctuation and grammar rules. It shows. Go on the websites of the people and companies that you admire and read their content. I guarantee you that the more professional the person, product, or service, the more flawless the content. Attention to detail goes hand-in-hand with professionalism.

I said earlier that I think that the phrase *thought leader* should be banned. I still do. In my opinion, the expression is very pretentious. However, there *is* room at the top, and those (few) people at the top *are* thought leaders. So, I'll concede this: If you master the rules of punctuation and grammar and use wonderful words correctly, as far as I'm concerned, you are on your way to the top.

And when you make it, I hope you'll see me there!

Sincerely, *Liz Coursen*

## About Elizabeth Huntoon Coursen.

Author, editor, speaker, and serial entrepreneur Elizabeth Huntoon Coursen (Liz) lives in Sarasota, Florida, where she owns several editing-, writing-, and publishing-related websites, including EditNATION.com, and LizCoursen.com.

Liz grew up in Sarasota, Florida, and Brunswick, Maine. She graduated from Emory University, where she put herself through school by starting a lawn care service and played ice hockey all four years—as the only girl on the team.

A four-mornings-a-week volunteer at a cat rescue (despite being more of a dog person), Liz enjoys vegetable gardening and hiking. Several years ago she started collecting books for homeless and needy people in the Sarasota community, taking in donations from libraries and individuals from all over Florida; so far, she has distributed more than 15,000 books to 11 Sarasota charities.

Liz is a two-club member of Toastmasters International, a former professional member of the National Speakers Association, and a regular lector at her church. She has presented workshops about American English best practices from Sarasota to Seattle, from Maine to Mumbai. Liz was once nearly kicked out of a WordPress conference for publicly airing her opinion about the so-called singular "they."

## A Book Wish List.

A couple of years ago I started climbing into library dumpsters to rescue discarded books. The first book I rescued was a paperback copy—completely readable and intact—of *Watership Down*, which is a total classic. I kept "dumpster diving" until the library threatened me with arrest, and then I started actively soliciting donations from (other) libraries and individuals. The Friends of the Alachua County Library has been especially generous—thank you.

I take the books I collect and distribute them to homeless and needy people in my community, mostly through nonprofits that work directly with people in need. I feel that literacy, the simple ability to read, just might be the issue of our time. Did you know that 24% of Florida's adults read at the third-grade level? I find that shocking and disturbing. Doesn't it follow that adults who can't read will have children who can't read? How are we, as a nation, going to be competitive if a substantial portion of our citizens are illiterate?

Below is a list of specific books I'd really like to distribute. If you can help, please email me. Reading is my favorite thing, and I bet you love to read just as much as I do.

**EVERYTHING BY MAX BRAND (MY NEW FAVORITE AUTHOR!)**

**Alas, Babylon—Pat Frank**

**Harriet the Spy, The Long Secret**, Sport–Louise Fitzhugh

**Thunderhead, My Friend Flicka, The Green Grass of Wyoming**–Mary O'Hara

**The Summer Birds, Charlotte Sometimes** (**early editions only**)–Penelope Farmer

**Gone with the Wind**–Margaret Mitchell

**Make Way for Lucia**–E. F. Benson (quoted extensively in this book!)

**Make Way for Ducklings, Blueberries for Sal, One Morning in Maine** by Robert McCloskey

Where the Wild Things Are, **The Nutshell Library**, Little Bear—Maurice Sendak

**Ferdinand the Bull**–Munro Leaf

**The Story about Ping, the Angus books**–Marjory Flack

**A Wrinkle in Time**—Madeline L'Engle

**Escape to Witch Mountain, The Forgotten Door**—Alexander Key

**Charlotte's Web**–E. B. White

Everything by P. G. Wodehouse

Everything by C. S. Lewis, especially **the Narnia series**, **The Screwtape Letters**

Anne of Green Gables series

Beatrix Potter/Tasha Tudor

**The Bronze Bow, Calico Captive, The Witch of Blackbird Pond**—Elizabeth George Speare

**Ben-Hur** by Lew Wallace

**The Bannerman series** by John Maxim

**The Tripod Trilogy**—John Christopher, plus the prequel

**The Prydain Chronicles**—Lloyd Alexander

All books by Stephen King, Jane Austen, Leon Uris, Arthur Hailey, James Clavell, Tom Clancy, John Steinbeck, Mark Twain, Pearl S. Buck, Robert Ludlum, Robert Frost, Bob Arnot, Shakespeare, Janet Evanovich, James Patterson

**The Hobbit, The Lord of the Rings** trilogy—J. R. R. Tolkien

**The Little Prince**—Saint-Exupery

All Marguerite Henry books (horse books for children)

All A.A. Milne books (Pooh)

All Walter Farley books (Little Black, A Pony; The Black Stallion, etc.)

Adrian Mole books–Sue Townsend

Plus, classics like Heidi, The Little Princess, National Velvet, Little Women, Treasure Island, Frankenstein, Dracula, The Three Musketeers, **Flowers for Algernon, Watership Down,** Valley of the Dolls, The Thorn Birds, Christy, King Arthur, Catcher in the Rye, Nancy Drew, the Hardy Boys, etc.

**Unlimited copies of all books by Dale Carnegie and Norman Vincent Peale**

Bibles in English and Spanish, especially the King James Bible

Self-help, leadership (Tom Peters!), public speaking, art, travel, how-to-read books for children *and* adults, history, humor, gardening, biographies, autobiographies, and magazines like *National Geographic* and *Toastmasters*

## Explanations about the sentences on the back cover.

**So wrong:** The Defendant is asking that the Court reconsider it's ruling.

Rule: *it's* is the contraction of *it is* or *it has*; the possessive of *it* is *its*. Ouch!

Corrected: The Defendant is asking that the Court reconsider its ruling.

(This was in the *judge*'s handwriting, so no blaming her law clerk!)

**Wrong:** Although the motion of MPP requests "a review of the record in BP-39", we limit the extent of our judicial notice as explained in this opinion.

In American English, quotation marks are *always* placed *outside* periods and commas. Hear my voice in your head: There. Are. No. Exceptions.

Corrected: Although the motion of MPP requests "a review of the record in BP-39," we limit the extent of our judicial notice as explained in this opinion.

**Wrong:** When a person is accused of a crime, how should they be seen in the eyes of a juror?

Rule: the noun must agree with its pronoun. "Person" is *singular*, but the pronoun "they" is *plural*. The good news is that workarounds are easy!

Correct: When a person is accused of a crime, how should that person be seen in the eyes of a juror?

Correct: After someone is accused of a crime, how should that person be seen in the eyes of a juror?

**Wrong:** 10 peremptory challenges are allowed for criminal defendants facing the death penalty.

Rule: Never start a sentence with a number, unless it is a year: write out the number instead.

Correct: Ten peremptory challenges are allowed for criminal defendants facing the death penalty.

**Wrong:** Let the jury know they will be excused early today.

Rule: "Jury," like "audience," "team," and "staff," is a collective noun and is singular, even though it refers to a group of people, and so you cannot use the plural pronoun "they." Again, the workaround is easy!

Correct: Let the jurors know they will be excused early today.

Correct: Let the members of the jury know they will be excused early today.

And this is just the tip of the iceburg! Oh, sorry. I meant *iceberg.*

Trust me, you *do* need this book.

Made in United States
Orlando, FL
06 November 2026

90299269R00144